KOREAN-AMERICAN CHRONICLES:

As Recounted by Korean High School Leaders

Hermit Kingdom Sources in Korean-American Studies (Number 2)
Series Editor:
Professor Onyoo Elizabeth Kim, Ph.D., JD
Han-Dong University Law School

Korean-American Chronicles:
As Recounted by Korean High School Leaders

EDITED BY
APRIL MYUNG

The Hermit Kingdom Press
Highland Park * Seoul * Bangalore * Cebu

Korean-American Chronicles:
As Recounted by Korean High School Leaders
(Hermit Kingdom Sources in Korean-American Studies, 2)

Copyright ©2010 The Hermit Kingdom Press

Hardcover (color) ISBN13: 978-1-59689-098-5
Paperback (color) ISBN13: 978-1-59689-107-4
Paperback (B&W) ISBN13: 978-1-59689-100-5

ISSN: 2156-2091

Write To Address:
The Hermit Kingdom Press
P. O. Box 1226
Highland Park, NJ 08904-1226
The United States of America

Library of Congress Cataloging-in-Publication Data

Korean-American chronicles as recounted by Korean high school leaders / edited by April Myung.
    p. cm. -- (Hermit Kingdom sources in Korean-American studies ; No.2)
 ISBN 978-1-59689-098-5 (hardcover : alk. paper) -- ISBN 978-1-59689-107-4 (pbk. : alk. paper)
  1. Korean American teenagers--Biography. 2. Korean American teenagers--Ethnic identity. 3. High school students--United States--Biography. 4. United States--Emigration and immigration. 5. Korea--Emigration and immigration. I. Myung, April.
 E184.K6K576 2010
 305.8957'073--dc22
                2010028592

Dedicated to Bergen County Academies

CONTENTS

INTRODUCTION

It was a great honor to be the editor of this important book that chronicles the lives of Korean American young leaders in the United States. I am very proud of the authors who have shared their life's experiences in this volume.

There are six future leaders who want to be medical doctors, who treat the poor and the sick. They want to make the world a better place through their lives and their lifetime of medical service. I also want to be a medical doctor, who helps those who are in need, so I can understand what moves them and drives them toward excellence. I would like to be a pediatric specialist in the area of Autism. My motivation has been, in part, my love for my family and my brother, who has been struggling with Autism. I want to help him and others who experience similar difficulties.

I am happy that there are future leaders who have contributed their life chronicles to this volume, who desire to make a real difference in the lives of those who are suffering. Besides the six future doctors, four of the authors in this volume are interested in becoming lawyers to fight for the causes of the underprivileged and the afflicted. I know that they will be great lawyers, who advocate on behalf of the oppressed.

I consider it my great honor to have served all the authors of this book as their editor. From the first day that we all met at a Korean restaurant in Closter, New Jersey, to the final compilation of all the chronicles, I am glad that I was able to get to know everyone on a personal level. As the editor, I have often taken a strong tone to prod the authors to make revisions, but all of them had been very receptive to my positive criticism. This has made my experience as the editor of the book a wonderful one.

I have learned a lot through the process of being the editor. I have spent sleepless nights, checking their writings with a view to improving them. I felt like I became a part of their life stories, as I spent so much time, reading draft after draft and observing developments and additions to their life stories.

My teachers at Bergen County Academies were very supportive of me, and I have to say that their support made me more proud to be a part of Bergen County Academies' community. I would especially like to thank my IB History teacher, Mr. Scott Demeter, and my IB Literature teacher, Mr. William Mendelsohn, and my AP Chemistry teacher, Dr. David Ostfeld, for their kind encouragement.

I would also like to thank Mr. William Hathaway, who was my faculty adviser as I learned how to be an editor of my high school newspaper, *The Academy Chronicle*. My experience as the editor of my high school newspaper certainly helped me in this monumental project. I would further like to thank my guidance counselor, Mr. Ken Zurich, who has been a beacon of light for me since the beginning, when I entered Bergen County Academies as a freshman.

Furthermore, I would like to thank my family members, who have been very patient as I strove to be the best editor. My mother, Eugenia Jeon, especially made significant sacrifices as she drove me to meetings and as she patiently listened to me whenever I needed a listening ear. My father, Nosung Myung, has been very encouraging as well, so I would love to thank him.

"Finding My Stride"
Julius Im

Before I begin the story of my life, I should start with my roots. My family, as far as I know, is mostly situated in Korea. My grandparents, much like other Korean grandparents, suffered the great divide between Korea and the war that ensued for 3 years in 1950-1953. Despite the difficulties and hardships of the war, my grandparents came through successfully in order to produce my parents, Hong Soon Im and Angela Im. My father, Hong Soon Im was a son of three children and my mother, Angela Im, a daughter of six children. Coming out of the Korean War, both my parents' families were not too well off financially. However, my paternal grandparents ran a business, which provided enough money to keep bread on the table. My maternal grandparents essentially lived on what was a farm, which helped them accumulate enough money to provide for my mother and her 2 brothers and 3 sisters.

My mother was skillful in her youth in several fields. She was the top runner in her school. Also, my mother was the top student in her school academically and possessed a very outgoing and playful image. My father had a love for music, inspired by bands such as The Beatles and Abba. He attempted to pursue a career in music, but even with this passion for a musical career, my father was limited by his friends, who parted and chased other careers. Nevertheless, my father's love for music did not stop; it was simply passed down to me, which explains my appreciation of music. In 1981, my mother and father met and after a few months they were married. Within 9 months my brother, A Shin Im was born in 1982. My father began a pool hall business in Jamsil, Seoul, Korea, the district in which we used to live. He was a successful pool hall owner and continued to operate it for several years. My mother was a homemaker because my father's pool hall attracted many customers and generated an income more than sufficient to support my family. However, when my family moved to the United States, he unfortunately had to pass down the business to his assistant and abandon his popular pool hall.

Shockingly, I was born ten years after my brother's birth, in Jamsil, Seoul, Korea. I cannot remember the first five years of my life as they must have been very insignificant. However, I do recall memories since I was six and beyond. At six years old, I was living in an apartment complex on the 14th floor and attending two kindergarten/preschool classes. I had many friends, but I could only consider two of those friends genuine friends.

One of my friends was the average cool guy, one that you might find in a Korean gangster film. He had the face, the hair, and the attitude of a guy who could really "talk the talk and walk the walk" and looked like he could smash a guy's face in in an instant even though he was just a kid at the time. I appreciated having a friend such as he because it raised my self-esteem. My other friend was a quiet type, similar to myself, but he looked like an intellectual. He was a kind and gentle being, one that didn't mind sharing his food whenever we ate and one that generally agreed and avoided arguments. I very much enjoyed the company of both of my friends and in school we were together most of the time.

My favorite memories with them are the several field trips my school took to the park nearby. The field trips were indeed my favorite because the days we went on the field trips were perfect; the days were clear, sunny, and the grass fields were indescribably green. We would have contests and my all-time favorite was grabbing the Werther's candy in a plate full of bitter flour, without using my hands. Of course, I really detested the flour and its bitterness because at that young age all kids want is something sweet. But what really drove me to suffer the flour was that sweet taste of the candy. After I attained the candy, I was so delighted that I got in line to do it once more. And after all that mindless fun, we all sat down in the grass and munched on some Korean delights, such as kim-bab and yubuchobab. Afterwards, we went back home, because everyone was exhausted from the activities and the food that we ate.

If there was anything I was inseparable from, it was definitely my Gameboy and Nintendo NES. They were my brother's possessions before I was born, and after he went abroad to the United States for our education's sake, his Gameboy and his Nintendo NES was handed down to me. I took the Gameboy everywhere, except school, because I actually had fun at school. The Gameboy was no ordinary Gameboy either; it was completely old school, one of the first Gameboys to be released. I would always play the same games over and over; Batman, Super Mario, Spider-man, and even one of the original cartridges of Tetris, with

the original soundtrack on it, despite the fact that I actually never knew how to play Tetris as a little boy. The Batman cartridge was one of my favorites; Batman was a very unrealistic Batman because he actually possessed a gun or ballistic weapon in the game that he used to vanquish the enemies. The most difficult level in the game, I would have to say, is when Batman is in his plane and attempting to fight all the impediments that the Joker sends after Batman. I could never defeat the heavy bombardments in that level and every time I was frustrated with that level, I asked my brother to complete the level for me. I can recall my brother defeating the game only once, and when he defeated the game, defeated THE JOKER, I almost pictured him to be godly because he had just defeated one of the greatest villains of all time. I thought that my brother was one in a million to have defeated the Joker and one of the best gamers ever, but that was, of course, proved wrong later on. The Nintendo NES was also a big part of my childhood because there were a lot of classic games I used to play. For instance, I played Ninja Turtles with 2-D scrolling as I role-played Leonardo, Raphael, Michelangelo, or Donatello. I never actually finished the game because every time I played the level involving defusing the bombs that were underwater, I would be too late to defuse the last bomb and the turtles were blown to smithereens (although it never showed it).

But, aside from the blissful times, I also had a near-death experience, which could have ultimately erased my memories and made this record non-existent. It was a cool summer night and my mom brought back groceries and a bag of one of my favorite sweets. I anticipated the sweet, sweet taste of the candy, and as the ball of sugar and flavoring and transparent appearance fell upon my tongue, a burst of gratification erupted from my taste buds. I savored the candy as I lay down on the couch while watching a cartoon on television, ignorantly.

I was enjoying the candy so very much, that as I sucked on it, it rocketed down my throat and became stuck in my windpipe. In a fit of panic, I jumped out of the couch, so that my dad did not even notice my spontaneous movement. I sprinted to my mother who was in the kitchen at the moment, and I jumped up and down frantically trying to make her comprehend my charade. Initially, my mother simply thought I was bantering; but she instantaneously realized that I was choking. She, just as equal in panic as

myself, began to yell for my brother and my dad, screaming that I was suffocating. My brother ripped open the refrigerator door as he tried to find something that could wash down the piece of candy in my throat. I chugged at least half a 12 oz. bottle of Pepsi, with no luck: the candy stubbornly remained lodged in my throat. My mother finally jammed her index finger down my throat in a brutish attempt to get the candy out of my throat. But alas, even this failed to prove successful. My mom being the resilient woman she was, tried again, and this time, she lay her finger on the candy and fortunately pulled it out of my throat. Everyone breathed a sigh of relief as I panted, and I was unbelievably thankful to survive.

On a typical day in Korea, strangers began to enter my house and to move the things in my house. There were packed bags sitting at the front door, and I was in disarray. I rushed to find my mom to inform her of what was taking place in our very apartment. All the toys I had collected were gone and the house was nearly empty. The piano was missing from its original place, and I could not find anything but my sofa and television. I rushed down all flights of stairs, 14 to 1, inclusive, to find on the yard, my piano completely trashed. The base was broken and the keys were everywhere. I thought to myself, "Why would we need to trash a perfectly decent piano?"

But even in the midst of all this chaos, I was actually somewhat excited because I didn't know what was ahead for me. Where we were going to go, I had not even the slightest idea. I had known previously that we were eventually going to move to the United States, but I had never realized how soon and abruptly the day would come. So, in other words, the day I moved out of my apartment in Korea utterly took me by surprise. My feeling about the move was very ambiguous as I wasn't sure whether I should be happy or sad. My thoughts at the time were something along the lines of, "Oh it'll be fun to move and

see new places," while this thought conflicted with – "Am I even going to come back to this town, ever? I haven't said goodbye to my friends, yet…" But as ambivalent as I was at that time, I had no voice to be considered by my family. I was not the head of the family; in fact, I was the youngest, so I had no choice but to follow my parents' decisions. So with my toys gone and nothing but a few necessary articles of clothing, I went with my mom to visit my teacher in school.

I sat in the office as my mother talked to my teacher, and as we were leaving, I bowed to my teacher, and she bid me farewell and wished me luck in the United States. Just like in the apartment, I was very ambivalent about the situation. I knew I was actually leaving my home country, but at the time, I had never realized how long I would be away. I was crushed at the idea that I would actually never come back to my hometown; yet, I still hoped that I would eventually come back and revisit all of my friends. Looking back at the abruptness with which moving to the United States came to me, I have immense regret that I did not give my friends a proper farewell or a last goodbye that was truly meaningful.

When I arrived in the United States, I stayed at my aunt and uncle's house. I could not speak the rudiments of English; the best I could do was "Hi". After a month or two, I entered the first grade at Thomas Jefferson Elementary School in Northvale. I remember my first day, entering the classroom; I was extremely unsure that I could actually do anything in the class, considering the fact that I could speak no English. However, I discovered that there was something fantastic for students such as myself: ESL, English Second Language—a class designed for students who learn English as a second language. Within a year, I had fully absorbed the English language, and I left the ESL class.

In the 2nd grade, I was fully proficient in speaking English independently, and I was proud of accomplishing such a feat. The 2nd grade was extremely enjoyable for 2 reasons: I met one of the greatest friends in my life, Jimmy Goetschius, with whom I share the fondest of memories, and I guessed the number of marbles in a jar correctly. Jimmy Goetschius is one of the greatest people I will ever

meet in my life. Since 2nd grade, we have ridden bikes all over the town, which has inevitably helped me to encompass my town and completely memorize the layout of my town. Today Jimmy stands by my side as one of my best friends whom I can speak to in Italian and talk about entirely exaggerated scenarios and make satirical jokes with.

The other reason 2nd grade was so great for me was due to my epic victory in a class contest. The situation was that there was a glass jar in which were several marbles. My teacher said to the class if any of us could guess the number of marbles in the jar right simply by looking, we could get a prize. I, for one, took the challenge, but I established the idea that I had a slim to no chance of guessing the number right as a fact in my mind. However, despite my doubts, I carefully analyzed the jar, absorbing the size of the jar and interpreting the circumference. I made an estimate of how many marbles were on the bottom, then I looked how high the marbles rose in the jar. I knew my methods of guessing how many marbles there were was highly unlikely to get me even the slightest possibility of guessing the right number. Despite the unimpeachable impossibilities of a right guess, I still went about trying to estimate a decent number and put forth my answer. Some students said 15 marbles, 26 marbles, 60 marbles, but I said 35 marbles. The teacher was just as eager as the students were to find out how many marbles were actually in the jar. So without further ado, she emptied the jar of the marbles, and began counting 1 by 1; one…two…three…it went on and on. Finally, it hit the thirties and I began to be hopeful that my number was actually the correct number. The final number came out to be 34. Even though my guess was an additional marble above the actual number, I was by far the closest to the actual number. However, someone in my class spotted a marble under one of the desks, and the resulting number actually DID come out to a startling 35 marbles! I was shocked and undeniably dismayed at the fact that I really guessed the number of marbles correctly. In my situation, I had just triumphed over an incredible feat; I had deemed the impossible as something possible. I felt like I was a god, that I was somehow omniscient and that I somehow possessed supernatural powers. Indeed, that was how satisfied I felt; it was almost as if I held the world in my own hands, my small second grader hands. From thence forth, I believed I could do anything and this euphoria was so extensive that I thought that I could walk in front of a car going at 60 mph and still survive the impact (which of course I did not do). However, it essentially gave me a new form of confidence, one that would compel me to take on even the most impossible challenges.

From 3rd to 6th grade, my confidence faltered mainly because of my physical appearance. Even as a 10 year old, I was extremely superficial and concerned a lot with my appearance. I despised the fact that I was "chubby," and I envied the kids who were "skinny". However, I perceived a golden opportunity to flaunt this envy: spring track. I challenged myself to train hard and truly make an effort to rid myself of the appearance of being "chubby". In 7th grade I considered track simply to be an exercise, a workout that I had never really explored before. It was undeniably difficult for me to run for even an hour and a half after school but it soon turned into something enjoyable and even a competition. After being involved in track for about a month, I realized it was not

enough to simply run. I saw the more competitive side of track; I needed to become one of the fastest runners in my school.

What inspired me was the legend of our school, supposedly the "fastest" in our school. I had never seen him outrun my friends, but he was apparently the fastest in the school. And by being the fastest, he had made a legendary name for himself. My friends were somewhere in the top with the "legend" who also inspired me to run harder. I almost saw the task of excelling in speed as an impossible feat just as I had seen predicting the number of the marbles in the jar to be. But similarly, I took on the challenge as impossible as it seemed. I sprinted as hard as I could during the practices but I suffered crushing disappointments as I could not match the top runners of my school. And because of this dilemma, I was unbelievably nervous every time a meet was to be held.

Despite my panicking, by the grace of God, every meet day was completely rained out, and we could not compete. For two or three months, every track meet, all but one, was rained out. The one exception happened to be the championship meet. I thought to myself, this is it—this is the chance I have to prove to myself that I have yet overcome another impossible feat. I ran in the 100 meter dash and the 200 meter dash, both of which I did not come close to placing first or second. I was slightly short of fourth in each race, and after the runs, I was fairly disappointed in myself because I had not proven what I had trained hard to prove. After the meet was over, I went home defeated and frustrated, thinking that this challenge that I had taken on was undeniably impossible.

What I did not realize at the time was the factor of patience. I could not see that the journey to attaining my goal was still underway, that it had not been finished; there was still another year to go. When I pondered my failure that day, I calculated in my head that 3 months of training was simply not enough; I needed to train hard, even in the summer, fall, and winter seasons if I really wanted to excel. With that thought in mind, I began to run consistently, training my body almost every day by running around my town. When school began, I commenced my arduous training by pushing myself to run every day. My middle school classes began at 8:40, which meant I needed to get up an hour earlier, so each morning I woke up at 6:30 or

even earlier, even in the midst of my drowsiness, quickly put some training clothing on, and walked out of my front steps and began jogging. When I began my training, it was undoubtedly very difficult to wake up so early and run for an hour in such drowsiness. However, as I progressed, 2 months, 3 months, and so on, I began to feel revitalization and relief every time I woke up and ran outside so early in the morning.

The most enjoyable part of my daily routine was the changing weather. In the fall, I received the winds and the sound of the leaves being dragged by the winds on the paved roads. The winter was my favorite because as I left in the morning to take my daily jog, occasional snowfalls occurred. When I saw the snow I was utterly delighted to see the white phenomenon cover the ground and create a cold and Christmas-like atmosphere. Moreover, I enjoyed the fact that I could experience such a morning for myself as if I were the only person to see this marvelous sight. It was almost as if I were in my own little world that no one could ever penetrate or pester me in. When I ran during those mornings, I felt isolated, but in a positive sense, that somehow helped me to train even harder. As I began to feel short of breath because of the frigid weather and my lungs gave out, I felt the need to push even harder. "Just up until the next block, and you can rest," I said to myself. I kept repeating this phrase until I could genuinely go no further. I stopped at an apogee of two times during my morning trainings in order to maximize my training. By spring time, I was confident in my skill and had no doubt that I improved. During my 8th grade year, I showed my tremendous improvement as I placed on an average, 2nd or 3rd in each race I participated in. And just as I had guessed the number of marbles in the jar correctly, I overcame the impossible task of making myself competent in track.

In addition to the feats I accomplished in 8th grade, I grew close bonds with a few spectacular people. In 8th

16

grade, the individuals that possessed the most influence in my life were Jeffrey Yoo, Roy Kim, and Danny Park. These three individuals were the closest of my friends with whom I made some of my best memories. I was already acquainted with all three individuals, but the 8th grade with them sealed my strong bonds with them. Almost every week, we hung out together at someone's house, whether it was Danny's house, Roy's house, or Jeffrey's house.

The majority of our time together was spent at Jeffrey's house mainly because we were able to engage in the most activities in his house. We all did a lot of things at Jeffrey's house, such as play Gamecube for hours without end, play Starcraft and Counter-Strike on his computer for hours without end, and jump on his trampoline mindlessly. Jeffrey proved to us that he was undeniably the master of games; in every Super Smash Bros. Melee game we played, Jeffrey was the victor. No matter how close to dying Jeffrey was with his avatar, he always managed to find a method to eliminate all the other players. It was especially amusing when I was a spectator because Danny and Roy became hopeful whenever Jeffrey's avatar had one life left, but in the end, Jeffrey simple obliterated Roy and Danny's avatars. In Guitar Hero II, he dominated and conquered every song there was in the game, missing at most 1 or 2 notes. I exalted him as a gaming god, and I was convinced that no other could challenge him. But despite the endless hours of gaming, my friends and I needed nutrition. To refill our energy bars, we ate Chef Boyardee's Ravioli, ramen, chips, and drank an endless supply of Brisk Iced Tea, Sprite, and Coke. Spending time with these three individuals was, indeed, a priceless period of time in my life because, for once, I felt like I was a part of something important and that I was a complement to this structure – and that without me the structure could not function.

In addition to these three individuals, I also met a very gifted teacher, Mr. Cebulash whom I refer to as Mr. C. When I first saw Mr. C., I first thought, "Oh great, he's going to pound us with work." I thought that I would loathe his classroom because that was simply the impression I got by looking at him. However, as the days went by in my class, I began to grow a liking to Mr. C. He was a very enjoyable person to be around, because he was someone you could talk to about anything. He had fascinating stories and each time he told one of his childhood stories, I would look at him with gleaming eyes and eagerly listen for the next word that came out of his mouth. There was this one story where he was in the car with his friend and his friend's mother, and a car swerved in front of the car. His friend's mother, in pure anger, rolled down the window and exclaimed, "WATCH WHERE YOU'RE GOING, YOU SON OF A BROOKLYN!" At the time he told the story, everyone laughed hysterically because we were at the age where curse words were an ultimate taboo and to use a euphemism such as "Brooklyn" was very amusing. Mr. C., I would have to say, was the best teacher I had ever met because I could really talk to him and regard him as a friend. Even today, I talk to Mr. C. occasionally because

he is still a great mentor due to his many years of experience in life and as a teacher.

As cliché as it may have been, I was nervous for my entrance into 9^(th) grade and the ominous high school environment. However, despite my nervousness I casually entered high school with a laid back attitude. The only "nerve-wrecking" scene I could have imagined in my freshman year was the senior class. The girls had make-up glamorously decorated on their faces and the boys had sternly built bodies, neither of which I could approach. Even though I saw such elevated physical appearances, I was indifferent to all these things around me. I went about high school as I saw it, simply "going with the flow". I did what I had to do, and that was that.

Perhaps, because of my indifferent attitude, I began to lose, what I believed to be, my identity. People often have a certain skill or trait that they can identify themselves with, whether it be a sport or hobby or interest. However, as I progressed through high school, I began to realize that I could not properly identify myself. In middle school, I could claim myself to be the best clarinet player in the school, a decent runner, and a good student; but in high school, that all changed because four different towns were all pooled into one school. I really could not match up to the kids in high school because their skills were further developed than my skills were. I was really lost because between my freshman year and sophomore year, I wavered back and forth between two groups of friends. In my freshman year, I was new to the school and was more accustomed to befriending English-speaking students. So in my freshman year, I was mostly around English-speaking friends, whether it was in or out of school. However in my sophomore year, I became better-acquainted with students that spoke my native tongue, Korean. I had not spoken Korean for some time, almost 10 years to be exact, but for some reason I was friendlier with my FOB (Fresh Off the Boat) friends and tended to get along better with them. My indecisiveness represented my lack of identity along with the idea that I had nothing else to identify myself with. I was really lost, and even my religious life seemed to falter. I began to lose sight of why I even attended church or why I even listened to the sermons that my pastor gave; I was spiraling into an abyss.

One day, as I shuffled through some old photos, I discovered the photos of my friends from Korea and the picnics I went on with my school. I found so much delight

because I could see our faces gleaming with joy, the youth, and the innocence in our hearts. Our faces were painted like cats and my "gangster" looking friend was on the left of the photo and my gentle friend in the middle and myself to the right. After eight years of leaving Korea and rediscovering this picture, I began to long for the things I had left behind. The true friendships and bonds that I had so foolishly taken for granted began to tear my heart apart. I was young and, of course, I took these things for granted! How could I not take them for granted? As terrible as I felt, I could do nothing about it. I could not go back to my home country; how could I? Until I was fourteen, I had spent eight years of my life learning English, reading English, and speaking English. I felt as though I could never return because my tongue had hardened in speaking the Korean language.

During the second half of my sophomore year, I began to attain my identity. One day, I was attending a club meeting when a classmate approached me and said, "Are you a Bboy?" A Bboy is short for "beat-boy" because he dances to the specific beat of a song; the cliché name for a Bboy is a breakdancer. I had always wanted to start bboying, but I never knew where to start. So, when my classmate asked me if I was a Bboy I wanted to say, "Yes," but, unfortunately, I did not have the skill to verify it. So, from that day forth, I began to bboy with my classmate, trying to use even the smallest bit of time to practice. For instance, after we finished our lunches, we would go into the stairwell and practice whatever we could, and even after school, we would try to practice for 15 minutes. I began to start watching videos of bboying on youtube, and I addict myself to the splendor and alien abilities of these bboys. For the rest of my sophomore year, I did not do anything productive in improving my skill because my classmate was not a pro at this dance, and I was a simple beginner.

My skill remained at a beginner level until summer, which was when I met my best friend Calvin Yim. It was during the summer of July 2009, that I met my friend Calvin at my church, Chodae. Chodae Church is perhaps the biggest Korean church in my part of Bergen County, New Jersey, with hundreds of high school students from grade 9 to grade 12. The reason I came to meet my best friend was because another friend of mine had suggested that we have a practice session in the gym at Chodae

Church, one Friday. I agreed and attended this session, which was exactly where I met Calvin. When I entered the gym, Calvin was already there, practicing and displaying his tremendous skill. I was astonished at the amazing ability of Calvin because never before had I seen a real bboy perform such spectacular moves. He had so much flavor and style to his dancing that he even influenced me. He showed me that bboying was not all about spectacular moves, but it was about feeling the music genuinely and celebrating the music even with the simplest maneuvers.

Calvin revealed to me the true world of bboying; it was about dancing and having fun and not impressing. Without Calvin, I would never have attained the true joy of dancing and instead I would only dance to impress with an empty motivation. I was thankful that Calvin found me, and from that day on, I became very close friends with him and began to practice with him, more often. And, as I practiced with Calvin, more friends came into my circle of friends; Andrew Yeam and Jonathan Cha were the few friends that I met during that summer and became close with. Calvin, Andrew, and Jonathan became my very good friends, and we practiced together whenever we could. As

I entered Junior year with a newfound experience of dancing, I began to conjure an identity that I could proudly stand by. Before I began dancing, I had tried other things, such as soccer, track, and Tae-Kwon-Do. However, I gave up on all those things, and when I started dancing, it was such a great experience and amazing way to express myself that I promised I would never give up dancing, not until I grew incapable of dancing or died. As I danced, I began to focus better; my religious view came back into line, and I began to try to understand the function of attending church and appreciating God and His love. My relationship with my family members and my friends grew even stronger, though my mother was initially against me dancing.

I continue to dance, today, and hope to stride to even greater lengths in improving my skill. I am truly thankful for the people I have met in the course of my life and the people I continue to meet and people I will eventually meet. I know I have definitely grown stronger over the years past and know that I will grow even stronger as I experience more hardships and impossibilities that I must overcome. But, despite knowing that I will have to face many more "impossibilities", I know that I can overcome these impossibilities with some help and guidance from God, and I acknowledge this because I have overcome impossibilities before as with the incidents in 2nd grade and 8th grade. I will be looking forward to the new adventures I will embark on and explore, whatever may be in store for me.

"Her Story"
Ruby Hong

Ruby Hong
Pianist

If I told you that she deserved everything she got, that would be a lie. It would also be a lie if I told you that she was happy all the time. Her life wasn't a fairy tale and she never got that fairy tale ending. She has met her fair share of villains and princesses while not even coming close to meeting her prince charming. Her friends were all magical, filled with unique powers and gifts, including her canine companion. She was not Cinderella, pure and sweet with nothing but good intentions; she was a human that had faults. She was not perfect and did not try to be but had determination that would overpower anybody's negativity. Of course, she wasn't strong all the time, but she was able to get back up after falling multiple times. Her mistakes were like rain drops filling up a puddle. That puddle eventually evaporated and became part of the beautiful rainbow. That is what she hoped to become, something extravagant, unbelievable, and a source of happiness.

Questions repeated in her head like a broken record player. Questions like: "Who am I, and what makes me, me?" Ruby Hong was a sixteen-year-old girl in a small suburban town, called Monticello, a town where the main street was slowly growing vacant and where walking was not the safest transportation. But no matter how much she didn't like the cracked sidewalks and sirens that wailed throughout the night, this town made her who she was, today. She grew up in this town for eleven years. The friends she made have also grown with her, and she saw how much this town had changed.

She was born in Passaic, New Jersey, a town that differed greatly from Monticello. This town wasn't crowded with one race or culture. It was not like the movie *Freedom Writers,* where it was a war zone between races. However, this does not mean that there was no racism. It was inevitable that wherever she went, somebody would point out the difference in her. If she was good or excelled at something, the excuse would be, "Because she's Asian."

She could never excel at something because she put her full dedication into it. People assumed that things came naturally to her, almost as if she possessed powers that were given to her by God. There were also instances when people would look down on her and especially her parents. Some cruel people would bluntly say that her parents needed to be educated. The thing was that she didn't understand why people had to meanly differentiate themselves from them. This town was racially limited, with few Asians, so if people saw somebody diverse they would treat them differently. Because of the constant segregation, Ruby constantly felt either superior or inferior to her peers.

Her parents were Korean, and she was a Korean American. Her father Sung Kak Hong was a South Korean citizen who immigrated to the Americas at the age of twenty-six. Ever since he was little, he was challenged to survive the world's fiercest situations. He grew up under his grandmother's guidance as his parents immigrated to the Americas to start a new life and to eventually bring something back from the place of great opportunities; well, that was the plan at least. After being separated from his parents at the age of ten, he grew up with the help of his aunts and uncles, with his younger brother. He was eventually reconvened with his parents after sixteen years. Her father's hometown was on plateaus and hills, where he had to constantly climb stairs to fetch water and do errands.

During his generation, Korea still suffered from the war, so the impoverished nation struggled to get back on its feet. Wages were low and kids played with what they got. With the lack of technology and bad economy, parents saved what they could and rarely spent any money on trips, toys, or leisurely activities. Her father reminisces all the time about his envy for rich kid's lunches and toys. They would have more to eat and especially with more incongruity. He would play soccer frequently because it was a sport where twenty-two people could play with one ball. Unlike baseball that required expensive equipment like leather gloves and metal bats, soccer's only prerequisite was one soccer ball. He was also covetous of the comic books that he could never afford. During that time, comic books became a disparate source of entertainment, so it was rising in popularity within the rich community. Ruby's father also has flashbacks about the times he was a carefree boy who splashed down rivers and creeks to catch fish. Whether it was eating or capturing fish, he enjoyed everything. The scrumptious dishes that incorporated whiting and fluke were able to put a delighted smile on his face. One of his favorite holidays was the Korean New Year. The special day served as a new beginning, but he particularly enjoyed

28

the money he received that day. As a blessing from elders, they usually gave money to their younger family generation as they bowed to them – offering them a rewarding and a blessed new year. In return, the money symbolized a prosperous future.

Her mother, Young Nam Jung, had a different family background from that of her father's. She lived in a household of seven. She had an older sister, younger sister, and two younger brothers. With the scarcity in food, sharing was essential within the household. When Young Nam was younger, her mother would rent out the rooms in her house, and the whole family would clutch over one another as they slept together in one room. As a young girl, Young Nam would protect her brothers from bullies and saved them during fistfights. For her age, she was always masculine and was talented when it came to games and sports. She favored marble and card games over playing with dolls. She set records of accomplishment in track at her school and was perpetually physically active. While growing up in the most highly populated city in Korea,

Seoul, she was never deprived from the city life. Malls and tourist attractions were huge in the area, so she has kept herself engaged. The most acclaimed and conspicuous schools were located in the capital, as well as large corporately owned restaurants. But with all the boisterous places and things the city offered, she did not have excessive amounts of extra money to spend on leisurely activities, like shopping at malls. Ruby's mother's favorite Korean dish was the traditional Kimchi stew. It integrated fermented cabbage into a spicy, warm stew. It would be surrounded with freshly picked bean sprout, tofu, and thinly sliced pork. It would have a relish of sweetness that overpowered the temporary spiciness from the powdered peppers deeply saturated in the stew. Next to her favorite dish was her favorite holiday, Christmas. In Korea, the Christmas spirit rapidly spread like an infectious disease covering the 37,911 square miles. She admired Christmas because when she was younger, it would be the holiday where she could spend unfathomable amount of hours with her friends. Now, Young Nam adores the holiday because of the giving mood that surrounded the gifts with the joyous carolers proliferating the positive Christmas spirit. She immigrated to the Americas at the age of twenty-seven after waiting three years for her green card. Only after receiving the card was she able to get officially married. As she reflects back on that time, she remembers the tedious and fervid times she wished the quiescence ended.

People tend to remember the hardest times of their lives. Ruby's father and grandfather consistently shared their stories of being in the army. In Korea, everybody was required to serve in the army for four years at the age of eighteen. They would take turns to make sure Ruby knew everything they did there. Whether the narrations included tedious, life threatening hikes up the mountains or cruel treatment at the base camp, they were not afraid to share the years when they suffered the most. Ruby remembers the time her father repetitiously narrated every chance he could get. In two-hour car rides to New York City or the fifteen-minute drive to work, he always made her remember that she had things easy.

After reading *The Things They Carried*, Ruby understood a little better about army life. She had thought her dad's stories were full of exaggeration and hyperboles to make things a little bit more interesting, but she came to realize that everything he said was indubitable and realistic. Picturing them running miles and miles with weights on their backs in burning, scorching weather made Ruby appreciate being a female American citizen. The small peninsula populated with millions of people had a long war history. After being seized by the Japanese and enslaved by their government, the Koreans never sought complete autonomy. Then, the communist war between the North and the South led to numerous causalities and suffering. The war concluded in neutrality, and the small nation was divided into two distinctive countries. The thirty-eighth parallel encompassed by soldiers from both sides was the division line between the communist and the democratic country. The mandatory military service required all Korean male citizens to be separated from families and loved ones. Even celebrities and singers were required to serve in the army; there was no exception. Ruby's father said that being in the army had made him the man, today. After surviving three years in the reprobated army, it was inevitable that soldiers came back as mentally and physically different people.

Their beginning adventure to the Americas was definitely not an easy or a pleasurable one. When people read immigration stories, they barely understand the difficulties they had. It also presents a biased side of the story because it only offers the hard working life of immigrants who soon became prosperous – who achieved that American dream. But what happened to the rest of the immigrants and their never ending journey to also achieve that American dream?

People come to America with the idea in their head that in this country anything is possible. In their inexperienced minds, optimistic thoughts, like "I could always get that four-bedroom house with a white picket fence," run through their head. But for her parents that dream house with that perfect family ceased to exist and seemed impossible when their immigration adventure began. With nothing but clothing and little money, Ruby's parents started out their marital life in a small apartment with rugged, old furniture. Their television was half disintegrated, and the food supply was not consistent. Bug infestation was only part of their problem when the water they drank was not sanitary. The apartment was hot, humid during the summer and brutal during the winter. They moved multiple times before they were settled with their first child, Ruby. Ruby's Korean name, Hong Minji, stood for "vastly understanding other people's desires." On her birth certificate, it stated, Ruby Minji Hong, to ensure her Korean heritage.

In the town of Monticello, Ruby and her family lived in a small two-bedroom apartment for five years. When Ruby was five to the age she was ten, she spent most of her childhood growing up at the Greenwood estates. There, she met many culturally and ethnically diverse individuals. Whether they were Caucasian, Asian, Mexican, Puerto Rican, or African American, it did not matter. There was no segregation when it came to friendly games of neighborhood kickball in the middle of the apartment's center field. The center field had flourishing cherry blossoms during the spring, complacent areas of shade during the summer, variegated leaves piled up in heaps in autumn, and anomalous snowmen during the winter. The center field was where the neighboring kids came together to partake of Easter egg hunts, snowball fights, baseball and soccer games. The boarder that surrounded the field was good for drawing with chalk, playing hopscotch, riding bikes and rollerblading. Even though the apartment in itself was not the most magnificent of places, the people and the surroundings were something that could never be

substituted. The neighborhood was an irreplaceable portion of Ruby's memories. She sat in front of her patio, traded Pokémon cards, and rode her bike with the other kids. She rode on the pegs of her older friend's bike as they sped past cars and people walking their dogs. Ruby and her siblings formed forts inside big pine trees and in between boulders. It was her own version of the wardrobe that led to Narnia. The recondite passageway to a tenebrous world full of purity and endless possibilities expanded her mind and imagination. Commodious boulders that could fit twenty people were placed in random parts of the center field. They became anything that Ruby wanted them to be, like rockets, cars, tortoises, or even a time machine. There was always somebody to play with and the kids were never weary. The energetic vibe from the adults and the kids enveloped the neighborhood and filled the households.

Born in the household of two parents who had laborious jobs, she never really had a chance to spend time with her family. She would see them exhausted after 12 hours of work, with their faces were full of boredom and pale from the loss of blood. Ruby would try to massage their parent's shoulders, but the excruciating pain from the exhausting work made it impossible to touch them anywhere without it hurting. The labor was as tedious as an assembly line; it was nearly impossible not to go insane. The pain that they endured to educate her and her siblings was gruesome. Ruby did not understand their position and sacrifice until she was 12, which meant that for the first 12 years of her life, she underestimated the idea of work and owning a store. The reason her parents moved away from the state where they had started the family was their economic status. It wasn't easy supporting a family of five with one parent working. Ruby's parents had one thing, and this was determination. This could be translated as being persistent, eager, and buoyant.

They started out as video store owners. The first couple of years went great because around the year of 1998, the world did not have companies like Netflix and movies on demand. With this store, her parents could take different shifts where each parent could spend time with their kids. Sometimes Ruby and her sibling would play in the back parking lot. They had scooters and roller blades, and they would continually play with them throughout the summer.

In the winter, they would go sledding down the slight ramp in the parking lot. There was a Chinese food place next door, so for most of their meals they would order from there. This store provided for meals and clothes. It was a place full of wonderful opportunities until the year 2005. Business became sluggish, and competition was rising.

New, big video stores were opening in town, and the number of rented movies and DVD's were slowly declining. Economically, her family suffered. This led to more arguments about financial plans and caused the family to slowly disintegrate. When her parents started a new farmer's market, the family unity worsened. The increase in stress caused her parents to take their anger out on each other, Ruby, and her siblings. The store was a lot of responsibility, as it was a bigger business that required more workers, time, effort, and experience. During the first year and a half, her parents grew distant to the point where at times they would sleep in different rooms and not talk to each other, sending messages through their kids. There were no discussions at the dinner table, and it was better if the house was quiet.

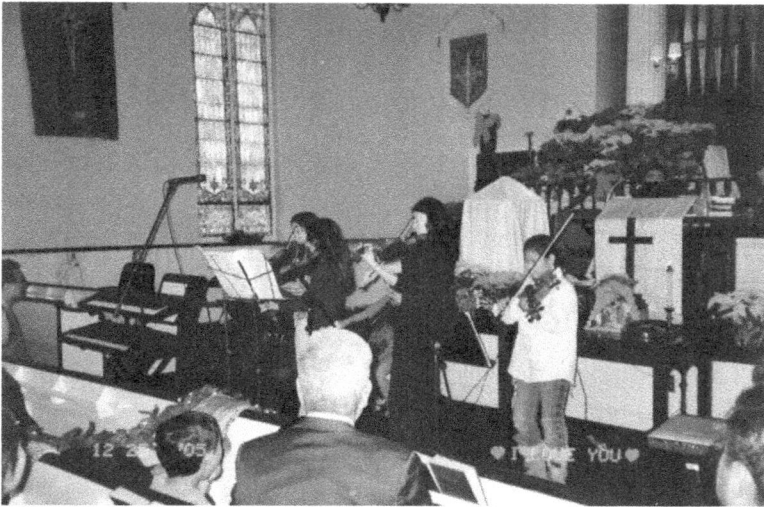

At times like these, Ruby and her siblings became closer. They slept together in one room, and a prayer was running through their heads, praying that this fight wouldn't lead to anything drastic. The three children who would constantly fight would get a sudden hit of reality when they realized that their parents could be divorcing. As much as Ruby hated the idea of her family breaking apart, the thought that her mother and father would be happier separate often ran through her head. It was then and there that weird scenarios ran through her head, such as what would happen if she lived with her mom, if her parents separated. Her mom hated living in America so she would immediately go to Korea, where Ruby would be separated from her siblings and father. At her wedding, her father wouldn't be there to walk her down the aisle. During Father's Day, there would be nobody to buy ties and power tools for. During Christmas, there would be nobody strong enough to carry the tree, and during New Year's, there would be a person missing from her New Year's resolution. If she lived with her father, Ruby would have nobody to look for guidance about boys and particular situations. She would miss that motherly figure that taught her how to cook and clean. The house would be quieter because there would be minimal discussion. However, after the store slowly gained popularity, the family disputes decreased significantly, ceasing these thoughts. Everybody was happier when things were economically sound. Because of her parents' situations, where their unhappiness was caused by their laborious jobs, Ruby decided that she would succeed at receiving an education so that she would never be in their shoes.

When things were not going so well in the house, Ruby would look at school as an alternative to get her mind off things. Monticello High School was the place where she would spend most of her day. It started with classes and ended with after school activities and performances in the auditorium. The school was almost like a barrier to what the real world had in store. For the most part you were safe. It offered things that other schools didn't, such as debate. Ruby joined the debate team for multiple reasons. Firstly, Ruby was shy and as quiet as a mouse. In middle school she rarely had any friends and just kept to herself. She didn't socialize with others and spent lunch in the orchestra

room. In grade school, Ruby would constantly be picked on for her physical features, which evidently led to a barrier between her peers and herself. Joining debate made Ruby get out of her shell. She started socializing, making new friends, and felt welcomed by the debate community. The students on the team were able to interact with students all over the continent and the team itself was a unity of different people that had a passion to do one thing. It's really ironic how she became a part of the debate team. It required her to be the opposite of whom she was, but it really just brought out the person that had been hiding behind verbal abuse and bad childhood memories.

The debate team was important to Monticello High School because it was not offered in many other places in Sullivan County and Orange County. Between the two counties, Monticello High School was one out of two high schools that participated in the National Forensic League. Because debate is a program that integrates a lot of traveling, expenses were typically above the budget that was provided. In order to make sure teammates were able to perform their highest potential, everybody on the team contributed their time and effort to make fund-raising a success. The debate team fundraised by completing an ad booklet in which team members would sell ads within the community. The completed booklet was distributed to everybody that purchased an ad plus all the debaters that attended the Annual Robert J. Kaiser Invitational. The team also raised funds with car washes. The collaborative effort and manual labor established a sense of unity within the debate team and an appreciative attitude to the value of work.

Each debate round was a new adventure, filled with different protagonists and conflicts. Analyzing opponent's debate cases required undivided attention to every single detail, author, definition, and source. There was no room for distraction because that one moment where you decided to blink was where you missed three words that came out of your opponent's speech. The intensity during a debate round was so thick that it felt like you were following the round in murky water. When Ruby had to hit debaters that qualified for the Tournament of Champions four times within the past year, her stomach filled with butterflies as if

they were desperately trying to escape. Her face blushed to a dark red and her ear temperature rose to a couple of degrees. Although everybody says, "Winning isn't everything," they are partially wrong. Ruby and many people realized the significance of winning. Without it, there would be no purpose to winners or losers. The consensus is that winning allows for many things. On the physiological level, the winner is able to come out of a round feeling accomplished and proud. They have more confidence in themselves, and they are extremely content with their achievement. Realistically, it allows the debater to have a more likely chance of entering the preliminary rounds and advances their amount of NFL points at a faster rate. This illustrates that winning does play a good substantial part of the debate round. The losers may have gained some ways to improve or fix mistakes, but the most annoying thing that resonates in your head continuously is the actual outcome of the round.

She was also part of the Nordic Ski team, which was a combination of hard-core training and skiing. Nordic skiing challenged her persistence and dedication because it was a sport where you had to challenge yourself to do and be better. It was one of the harder sports in the school because firstly nobody on the team originally knew how to do Nordic. It was one of the unpopular sports where it required a lot of individual training. It required self-discipline and effort which a lot of people lacked. But by being on the team and experiencing something that required so much hard work, Ruby was able to recognize her full potential and how things aren't just given to you and that some things people have to work for. Coach Fitchett directed the team in warm-ups and skiing. Because Nordic Skiing was so rare in this county, the coach had to teach new comers every year. He displayed patience and persistence when some teammates took half of the season to learn the sport. He offered his skis and poles to anybody who could not purchase their own. Coach Fitchett displayed a very warm welcoming hand and encouraged the team to do better. After laps around the course, the coach would constantly be chanting for the team's victory from the starting/finish line.

One thing that Ruby particularly favored was music.

She likes the fact that music could express what words couldn't and how the form could bend, twist, and do loops into whatever you wanted it to do. She liked how sometimes playing silence was almost music where it was a natural form of beauty.

She related life to music as if it were a big metaphor. It had its crescendos when things were climatic, and, sometimes, things were in slow motion, almost like during a retardation. Music made up her life since the age of seven. She started piano lessons from one of her Mother's friend, and she gradually received lessons from a formal piano teacher, Ann Trombley. Mrs. Trombley was another motherly figure to Ruby. Ever since she was in fourth grade, Ruby would stay at her house to attend weekly hour lessons. Because Ruby helped Mrs. Trombley teach young musicians about the essence of music theory, she would sometimes be at her house for hours. As she grew older, more music opportunities were available. She participated in many community service centered music performances. Whether it was in school or at the Trombley studio, the students constantly took part in the community. Ruby and her classmates would play music for the elderly in the hospital, perform for various art shows, and give performances in buildings after pitching in hours of community service to fix up old auditoriums. Ranging from variations to sonatas, Ruby was challenged to do her best. She constantly performed on the piano, which led to a decrease in stage fright and a friendlier vibe when thanking people for their support and compliments.

Another program that was advantageous to where she lived was the Weekend of Chamber Music internship. Ruby participated in this wonderful event when she was a freshman in high school. She was part of a quartet with a flutist, cellist, violinist, and her on the piano. The busy summer called for Ruby to attend rehearsals and practice constantly. The internship consisted of receiving very valuable chamber music guidance from the people of the Weekend of Chamber Music. Each musician would receive a couple of private lessons with well-known musicians. Every weekend over the summer, the Weekend of Chamber Music would have other musicians around the continent or the world to perform for the local community. The concerts consisted of varied music that was rarely heard and a new experience that was not available in the city. The barn-like building in the vast open green lawn contributed to a

completely different vibe when listening to the chamber groups. It was definitely an unforgettable and priceless experience to be coached by some of the most well respected musicians.

During the summer of 2007 and 2008, Ruby participated in the Shandelee Music Festival. The Festival wanted to incorporate the community, so it established a day camp for a couple of individuals living near the area. After passing auditions and the interview, Ruby was able to attend one of the most cherished events of her life. Even though Ruby lived in the suburbs, the Shandelee Music Festival's campus was more than extraordinary. The big open green fields with a small pond and various berry bushes contributed to the amazing scenery. The waterfall like entrance along with the pool and tennis courts made the place even more unbelievable. The festival also had the best baby grand pianos to practice. There was trail of four cabins where the students could practice. The four cabins each had a Steinway baby grand piano and were separated by a good number of feet, so musicians could practice in an isolated area where they were free from distractions. The trail was developed right in the woods where pianists would be practicing around Mother Nature. Woodland and forest creatures would peep out of their habitats to come listen to the enriching sounds produced out of the Steinway pianos. While walking up to the trail to the assigned cabin, Ruby was able to think about everything and anything. The peaceful setting and isolation from busy streets and people gave her a chance to contemplate and reflect about the possibilities in her future. Each musician would receive a schedule directing him or her to when and where things were. It outlined the times for lunch, practice, concerts, and lessons. Everybody had a minimum of four hours to practice a day and at the end of the summer, the musicians would perform for the community. The students attending the festival received lessons from a well-known piano teacher, Yelena Mamonova. Because the Summer International Artist Program occurred during the same time, Ruby was able to meet pianists from all over the world. Their talent and passion for piano was inspiring, and their dedication to practice was rousing.

Ruby started the viola at the age of 10, when all students in our elementary school had an opportunity to pick an instrument. Everybody in her music class was compelled to pick well-known string instruments such as the violin and the cello or even popular band instruments like the saxophone or the flute. For some reason, Ruby does not know why she favored the viola. She didn't have any outside influence from her parents and so Ruby was completely accountable for the instrument she picked. The viola mostly resembled her personality. In history the viola doesn't have original compositions made for the particular instruments but when it is played it has a vibrant sound that echoes throughout the halls and rooms. It may look like it was an unworthy opponent compared to the violin and cello but it had its moment to shine. Music made up her life, literally. She would perform in musicals, be accompanists for choirs, sing, join music internships, and play in piano festivals, and participate in chamber groups. The small suburban town had a lot to offer and she used it to her advantage.

Ruby's sister and brother also played instruments. Her sister, Esther, learned piano when she was five and the cello when she was ten. Her brother, Stephen, learned the violin when he was also ten. One of their mother's dreams was for her children to form their own trio. The problem was that it was going to take a while before Stephen and Esther could play fairly moderate pieces. Esther was a unique individual. Actually, she was the complete opposite of her sister. She enjoyed shopping for those brand clothes like Hollister and American Eagle that seem to be so popular today, and she was more of a girly girl that focused

on her nails and hair. Her range of friends differed, and she tried immensely hard to fit in with the group of friends.

Even though some people do not think that social hierarchies exist in school, they have a misconception. Esther was placed into those hierarchies, and it was hard for her to come out of it. She tried a lot to please people, and she naturally became extremely blunt. Her attitude resembled somebody who was constantly looking down on herself until she found the group of friends she wanted. Middle School was hard for her because her peers had these irrational thoughts that race was everything; ignorance is inevitable in some situations. Stephen was ultimately the cutest out of the three. Although he did lack in the academic side, he was the most creative. Ranging from building legos to experimenting with circuits, he always had something to build. He hung out with the older guys, sometimes with people who were four years older than him. Everybody had talent, and when one person lacked in something, the other person helped. Esther was very opinionated, and so she didn't mind what people thought about her. She was not afraid of public speaking and had a rather loud voice. Esther was a singer who participated in all the musicals and talent shows and attended music festivals for voice. She had a passion for singing and people passionately listened to her. Ruby's siblings influenced her to be the person she is today. Whether they are extremely annoying or incompetent, she looks beyond that and just reflects back on how much they make up her life and how they are an irreplaceable component of her life.

Since the age of eight, Ruby and her siblings would attend the day camp in her town; Town of Thompson. The camp offered many things and established a sense of family to those children who lacked some paternal attention. Camp counselors and counselors in training became like older sisters and brothers. Campers felt safe and happy. Even though Town of Thompson Day Camp was not flourishing with endless money for weekly field trips, campers had the best time there. Ruby enjoyed the playground, and as the years progressed, the playground's moderation fulfilled her contentment and satisfaction. The big slides, multiple swings, labyrinth-like jungle gym and the balance beam made the moments there even more memorable. Ruby and her friends would start tanning on the woodchips of the playground or eat lunch on the balance beam. They would play tag on the jungle gym or play hide-and-go-seek behind the hidden trails. She would have competitions with her friends to see who could swing the highest or who could reach the leaves on the trees with their feet.

One unforgettable landscape that made the day camp so unique was its hill. The hill sloped down so that it was almost like a vertical wall. Climbing up that hill was a torturous exercise. When Ruby was littler, she and her friends would have races trying to climb to the top. It was a place where they could roll down the hill and where they could soak in the sun. At the end of the day, the hill became the destination where all campers ranging from the ages of five to twelve would sit and wait for their parents to pick them up. The fields at the camp were enormous. It was big enough so that each age group could have their own private area, and it was just small enough where campers could not get lost. The camp also had a five-foot deep pool donated by a caring family. Before the pool was installed, the campers would hike to go the water hole. There would be a capacious boulder big enough to fit twenty people. It was the post for the lifeguard and served as a diving board as the kids jumped into the water. Ruby remembers getting wet sand between her toes and mud on her bathing suit as she climbed her way out of the water. Deep in the woods behind the water hole filled with rambunctious campers splashing around were salamanders. The campers loved to search for orange-colored little newts that scurried across wet moss. Activities like color war and camp Olympics always made the campers filled with gaiety. Campers were divided into teams and were responsible for coming up with cheers, dances, and winning points from games. The couple of weeks were filled with intense competitiveness as everybody, even the counselors, entered the patriotic mood. The camp offered copious things that diverse people could do in their own time. Each camper could do what fitted his or her fancy. If sports were not their particular hobby, the camp had a time for arts and crafts and a time for playing.

The town also had a soccer program, called American Youth Soccer Association. During the fall season, Ruby and her siblings would actively participate in this sport. The favoritism toward this one sport might have been hereditary, but it was something that the three siblings loved to do. AYSO allowed them to make new friends and increase their competitiveness. At a young age, the game of soccer was following the leader. Little munchkins with cleats, shin guards, and soccer jerseys ran from one end of the field to the other as they tried to get the ball into the goal. To them, positions in the field did not matter as long as they did not use their hands, kept it away from their goal, and tried to get it in their opponent's goal. The game of soccer was simple at the age of eight. It was a nonviolent, amiable, dynamic sport where each individual had an equal and fair chance of playing. Ruby had a weird obsession towards soccer. It steered away from dolls and playing house and let her play a team sport. It showed her sportsmanship and the importance of encouragement. Being egotistical and selfish was not a favorable characteristic in the game so she learned the essence of sharing such as passing a ball.

Ruby never feared to get dirty or physically hurt. She loved the rush of adrenaline pumping through her veins and the sweat dripping from her forehead. Being active, competitive, and hyperactive was what Ruby admired about life. She always pictured herself doing some crazy things, like parachuting or bungee jumping, but her friends did not feel the same way. They loved to be on the safe side, preferably away from danger as much as possible. The reason why she revered danger was that she favored challenges. Whether the challenges were physically or mentally difficult, Ruby never backed down easily. She challenged herself when it came to individual sports and made sure she made improvements. This was evident in her piano skills, track long distance times, ski records, and New York State Schools Music Association viola scores.

Because her parents worked constantly, Ruby never took a trip out of the tri state area for a family trip or vacation. Just when her life could not get any duller, her best friend Gabriela Garcia and her family offered to bring Ruby on their family trip to Florida. There, they rented a house for a week and met up with the rest of the Freestone family. The twenty-four-hour, nonstop drive in a pickup truck with five people was not a pleasant trip. The pit stops for three-hour naps in the middle of the night did not satisfy the driver or the passengers. Luckily, everybody made it to

Florida in one piece. When the truck pulled up into the driveway of their Florida house, the kids just stared at it with awe and excitement and could not wait to step into the warm tropical weather. The tinted yellow house had a heated pool, Jacuzzi, 7 bedrooms, a living room, a dining room, kitchen and a pool table. The staircase was lined up in the middle of the entrance and the furniture just glistened and sparkled. The house was bigger than what Ruby could have ever imagined.

During the first day, Ruby and the family went to The Sea World. They saw marine animals, including the infamous killer whale, Shamu. The performance they put on left Ruby speechless, as the whales swum and worked alongside the professionals. The moving screens in the background lit the dark sky and displayed unforgettable pictures, quotes, and music. The overall capturing scenery made it impossible not to pay attention. The whole thing was so alluring to a small suburban town girl. The next day, the family ventured to The Animal Kingdom. The park immediately succeeded to impress Ruby, as multiple and varying animals were placed in designated areas around the entrance. The prodigious tree of life had carved in animals on its trunk. The arduous, intricate, and realistic carvings were relatively similar to the actual size of the animals, and inside of the tree was a theater where they performed with the surround-sound system and underground acoustics. The Animal Kingdom also had a safari where people could observe the animals in natural habitats, only a couple of feet away. The elephants sprinkling themselves with water were definitely a picturesque image. The flamingos perching on one leg and the lions yawning while basking in the sun were also unforgettable highlights of the day.

The next day was the trip that Ruby yearned for the most. They were finally going to go to The Disney World, where they had the magic castle along with the Disney characters that Ruby only saw in videos when she was a kid.

The moment she entered through the gates was when she finally realized her inner child was trying to escape free. The advertisements on television were not misleading when they said that everybody could fit in. Even though she was fifteen, in high school, and very mature for her age, her overexcitement at seeing Mickey Mouse was priceless. Riding Disney attractions and going through the haunted mansion provided a feeling of accomplished dreams and goals in life. She rode Dumbo as he flew in the air and saw the parade that was bright enough to light a city. As she slowly approached the blue and silver castle, she could not control her excitement. Jumping up and down, she was more excited to see the characters around the magic castle than the five year olds on their parent's back were. Taking trips to park attractions halted for a day as the Ruby and the Freestones enjoyed a big Thanksgiving feast. Waking up early in the morning, Gabby's mother, grandmother, and aunts prepared the turkey, mashed potatoes, pumpkin pie, and other essentials during a Thanksgiving dinner. The event was an effectual, gratified, and cherished family dinner as everybody around the room shared their thankful thoughts. The last days were scheduled for the Tampa beach and/or MGM and Epcot. The day that the rest of the Freestones decided to soak in the Floridian sun, Gabby and Ruby decided to go on their own adventure and visited another Disney Park. The vacation finally came to a slowly diminishing ending as the drive back required twice the time it took to get there. The long line of traffic between the four southern states stretched all the way past Washington D.C. The uncontrollable anger while driving was presented to little kids in the cars, and the lack of manners in congested vehicles made the end of the trip unforgettable.

Every Sunday, Ruby would attend church. The forty-five minute drive weekly was definitely worth the trip. Many people contemplated about what it really meant to be

Christian. Whether it was to follow the Ten Commandments, to not commit any sins, to listen to the word of God, Ruby found out the answers there. At this holy place, she was able to find a group of kids and pastors to help her through what it really meant to be a Christian. Each sermon and scripture in the Bible was shared for the growing young minds that followed God's path. As curious teenagers, they constantly asked questions that would enhance their knowledge and understanding. The church allowed the kids to attend retreats during the winter and the summer. It was a big collaboration that incorporated big churches all over the tri-state area, where Korean American Christian kids could gather and spend a couple of days together, learning and experiencing the words of God. At times, it would get very emotional during prayer, and it would get physically intense during outdoor activities. It was an enjoyable activity for the people attending to get to know different people that had a similar perspective on things. After retreats, Ruby would make numerous amounts of friends to whom she could go, to ask for guidance and advice about certain issues.

Church was a community within itself. Everybody helped each other and depended on one another. Trust and loyalty was established between relationships, like in the book, *Seedfolks*. Everybody's garden was his or her own knowledge, trust and belief in God. People helped one another grow, protect, nourish one another's "garden." It was a place where worries diminished to a certain level, where it was not constantly on your mind. The church offered many programs, too. It established a Korean school, where it made sure the generations born and raised in America did not forget where their heritage was from. The academy taught kids the Korean language. It established levels that differentiated each individual's skill. Adults volunteered to teach the kids and the older students volunteered to help the children. The church had their own

praise team, composed of kids like Ruby's age, to play in front during worship time. The band consisted of string and band instruments with piano accompaniment. It required dedication and effort when it came to coming to rehearsals and practicing. For some people attending church every week was a boring and tedious chore, but to Ruby attending church was like going to a second home. It was not a bother to her, nor have she ever considered it as an obligation.

The Hudson Valley Korean Methodist Church decided to expand their Christian influence by deciding to participate in a mission trip to the Dominican Republic. Ruby knew that this would be a life-changing experience because it was a time where she could spread the knowledge she had about God and his word. It was also a time for Ruby to clearly see the world beyond the walls of Sullivan County. She hoped to learn many things. Although she was going to be a missionary, she felt that she could also learn from the Christians and non-Christians in the Dominican Republic. Seven Christians along with their pastor would be in Dominican Republic for a week exploring, teaching, and learning in a different environment. The trip would include visits to rehabilitation centers and

Korean churches. It also incorporated physically interacting with the community by spending nights at other people's homes. The missions trip required a lot of practice. The group was required to learn twenty songs in Spanish along with their dance and a skit based upon scripture. Even with the hard work that was required for the trip, it did not diminish the amount of excitement for Ruby.

Have you ever dreamt of being somebody or something that exceeded what the imagination could generate? Have you ever had goals that did not center on anyone else's expectations but your own? It was really hard for Ruby to be independent when it came to her future. Being the first generation in America, the world of opportunities, her parents sought the best and provided what they could for her success in the future. Every Korean American is forced to be the best. There is no exaggeration, as being second is not an option. Although, this helped her strive in this big competitive world, it also left little room for failure. This made Ruby fear the consequences of failure. However, through life experiences, she realized that even with mistakes, there is still room to succeed.

Ever since she was little, Ruby had a lot of dreams, ranging from those of being a vet to an individual that traveled around the world to save endangered animals to becoming a marine biologist and to even imagining being an artist. Kids have a lot of dreams of what they want to be, such as the president of the United States. Ruby had numerous goals, and she just wanted to be that wonder woman that could do everything, but when she started to grow up, she realized that she had to choose a certain career. Growing up in this town, she witnessed many individuals that could not receive the help that they needed, especially the help that related to their health. In her home, her parents sacrificed many trips to the hospital to save money from the lack of health care. Their pain and the suffering they endured really pushed Ruby to be an individual that made a difference in the medical field. By becoming a doctor, Ruby felt and knew that she could help individuals like her parents and assist with their pain and suffering. Ruby also considered traveling overseas to impoverished nations, like in Central America, to help them receive medical assistance. Ever since Ruby was little, she saw the dangers of money and the change in personality that came along with it. The superiority complex in some people after becoming people, like doctors and lawyers, was unbelievable. After witnessing arrogant, selfish, braggart individuals, Ruby hoped to become an individual that contrasted from all those negative characteristics. She hoped to become a doctor because it would be a way to help the most people and not because it would generate much income or popularity. Whether people knew her name or not, Ruby really did not care. As long she was able to aid those in need, her life would be filled with contentment, happiness, and a sense of success.

In order to expand her knowledge about the medical field, Ruby decided to volunteer at a hospital. By actively watching and helping patients and nurses, she had a chance to familiarize herself with the environment. Nurses and doctors whispering to each other made it seem like they had something to hide, almost as if they were the bearers of bad news. The phone constantly rang for soon-to-be-mothers in the labor room or for nurses to discuss the status of patients. The hospital staff was very kind, even to patients who seemed to lack manners. Even when the elderly spit food in their faces, they prevented themselves from acting inappropriately or uncivilized. Being a good nurse was hard at times when patients did not want to listen. It made things extremely difficult for the people on shift because it would just be an extra unnecessary burden. Ruby learned that being a doctor or just even entering the medical field required a lot of patience; patience for lab results to come back, patience for the behavior of others, and patience for time. Everything had to be clean and organized because there was no room to mess up. Tidiness was the key to being efficient. Whenever Ruby had a chance of spare time, she would organize equipment in rooms and stock up materials in the storage room. To make things easier for the nurse staff during their busy schedule, Ruby tried to make beds, pass out water to patients, and organize files for them. The staff in the hospital considered their health before they bought something from the cafeteria. They had hesitation before they picked up the Boston crème donut from the Dunkin Donuts box. Whenever Ruby would unintentionally listen to their conversations, they would be talking about the exercise they did or that they needed to do. Being on the hospital staff, they had a big realization and understanding of what their lives could lead to without exercise. The patients that entered through those hospital doors because of poor eating habits served as a deterrent for others.

Being a Korean American consisted of a lot of different values and customs. Ruby went to Korea when she was one and three years old. At this age, she really could not absorb and get to reflect the life of Korean people in their community. Ruby was curious about what life in Korea would be like; how their education system varied from the Americas, how the students' life style was different, and how Korea's economy stood. She knows that her parents gave up happiness, comfort and family in order to come to a foreign place for her future. She wanted to exactly know what made her ethnic Korean side so unique and important to her. Growing up in the town that she did, her household rarely celebrated traditional Korean holidays. The values that surrounded America and its holidays were more active in her household than Korea's values and customs. But Ruby's parents were exploding with Korean patriotism and shared with her numerous stories that expanded Ruby's knowledge of Korea's history and traditions. Because her parents have not been to Korea in the last thirteen years, a lot that they know have changed. The modern viewpoint of its culture and environment was excluded from her parent's stories. Instead, stories about the poor and pre-technology times always ran through Ruby's head.

Living in the Americas for more than ten years still did not change her parent's Korean ways. At home, the family would still have its Korean side dishes and rice. Everybody would still eat with chopsticks and spoons and consider soup a very important part of dinner. Kimchi was a necessity during every meal because the pureblooded Koreans in the household could not survive a meal without it. Her parents never forgot to share their experience with delicious encounters with Korea's finest meals and dishes. These stories really wanted Ruby to hop on a plane and go to Korea. Its range of seafood and spicy but delicious dishes made Ruby's mouth water. Although these dishes were available in America, her parents explained that it was never the same to the way it was made in Korea. Ruby's possible lifestyle in Korea ran through her head. She pictured being the same as everybody else and the benefits it would bring for not being different. Then, it came to her realization that she liked being different. Her diversity from others made her value her culture even more. Even though it did bring struggles in her life, as she was growing up, the lessons that she learned from these unpleasant experiences were worthwhile. She loved being one of the few Asians in her town and she cherished the idea of being rare. They tried to describe the life in Seoul, Korea and it was just impossible to picture. Living in the suburbs did have its disadvantages. Ruby never experienced that busy city life where riding the subway and the bus was a natural part of her day. She could not picture walking around alleys and roads that looked all the same, and with the immense amount of traffic, she slightly felt overwhelmed.

But no matter what headed towards her direction, her parents said to never give up because once she did, there was no room for success. Life had its moments of undeniable moments of happiness and predestined trials of sad, miserable times. This autobiography allowed me to analyze the world that surrounded the view of her and others through a different perspective. The alternating view made it possible for Ruby to finally realize the truth in her own reality as well as her futuristic viewpoints that articulated her goals and dreams. The realization and progress that Ruby has gone through something that I could not see. But once Ruby stood in front of the mirror and started to question what the reflection was actually presenting, I received a different but more personal answer, every time.

"My Discoveries"
Andrew Hyeon

"Your body can go farther than your mind says it can." This is what our coach tells us as he conditions us for the football season. I have seen that this is not just for sports, but it affects all parts of life. Most things take mental strength more than anything else. Waking up at 5am after a late night doing homework, going in the morning to the next day of preseason football with sore muscles, starting your night of studying when you know that you are going to be up all night, or even playing hard for the last quarter of the football game are all more than just physical challenges. They force you to become mentally strong, to fight against your mind to be able to overcome your weaknesses. From what I have learned in the past couple years of high school, life is all about being able to overcome the limitations that your mind sets and to just move forward.

I am a sophomore attending the prestigious Hopkins School, and I have been blessed to have met great people and to have experienced many things. Born as Dong Sup Andrew Hyeon at St. Vincent's Hospital in Manhattan, New York, My long journey has finally led me to my high school in New Haven, CT. I moved to Connecticut at age 3 and moved from Danbury to Brookfield and finally settled in Newtown.

Founded in 1660, Hopkins School is one of the oldest educational institutes in the US. As a school that dedicates itself to the "breeding up of hopeful youths", it has successfully educated many of its students to become great members of society. The school follows its mission well and ranks 19th in the nation's top prep schools. With famous alumni like Edward Bouchet, the first African American and the sixth American ever to receive a PhD in physics, Walter Camp, the founder of American Football, Josiah Gibbs, the founder of thermodynamics, and Harold Koh, the former dean of Yale Law School and the current Senior Legal Advisor to the State Department of the US, the Hopkins School has a distinguished tradition and legacy for us students to continue.

I set foot on Hopkins for the first time during football preseason. For those who don't know about football preseason, it is basically hell on earth. Those two weeks of pain, torture, and endless running helped me forge strong friendships with my fellow football buddies. Keith, Tikim, Arya, Luke, and I slogged through tackling practice, blocking drills, and conditioning, wondering what we had done in our previous lives to deserve something like this. Coming in on the first day might have been the scariest thing I have ever experienced. Not knowing anybody, and expecting to play a contact sport with high schoolers for the first time was an intimidating prospect. What made it worse was that since this was my first time playing, I had no idea what was going on.

The first practice seemed easy. Doing some light agility drills and conditioning allowed me to get to know some of my teammates. But that practice was nothing like the rest of the week. Slogging through tough drills, getting hit all the time, and the running – our mental and physical states were besieged for two long weeks. It took a herculean effort to survive all the running done in pads, out of pads, while practicing tackling on any afternoon in the middle of August. After every strenuous practice of preseason where we worked muscles we didn't even know we had and boiled inside thick layers of pads, there was conditioning. This meant sprinting at a full speed back and forth for numerous yards multiple times. And to make it worse, once that day was over, we had to come back the next morning sore and tired to endure the same things over and over again. For those two weeks, we suffered as a team, practicing mornings and afternoons in 90 degree weather. There was a point where it was so hard that I thought about quitting. I was new to the sport, and the sheer amount of work and effort needed was almost too much for me to give. Every day I just told myself, "just a little more" and I was able to endure those two weeks. Completing those weeks in hell made me enjoy life all the more. I could truly enjoy lying back content.

Then school started. Thrust back into the reality of school and into the new idea of a high school life, I started classes at a school where half the kids had been together for two years. With the other, new, half of the student population, I walked in with wide eyes. Large buildings and a sprawling campus on "the Hill" both impressed and daunted me. I was taking my first steps up the stairs, and I tripped. That is how I began my Hopkins experience. With such a foreboding start, I had expected high school to start badly, but I was able to make new friends and quickly became accustomed to the new school environment. Even though I had to walk a marathon to get from class to class, I learned to love my life at Hopkins. Great teachers, engaging classes, and a friendly community all made me love being at school. But my life at Hop is just the culmination of this story.

For much of my life, I never really had a plan. I just went with the flow, and somehow I ended up here at Hopkins. I guess it all began back in the March of 1994 when I was born. I grew up in Danbury, Connecticut where I spent my days going to kindergarten at St. Peters and watching Pokemon when I got home. I moved to Brookfield in 1999. Brookfield was heaven for me. I lived there from first through fifth grade, and I spent the days accompanied by many of my friends, playing baseball, pulling all-nighters while playing Halo with Jake, and goofing off in class. Contrary to the usual stereotypical kid, I loved school. I didn't think of school as a place where I had to go to take boring classes and study, but I thought of it as a place where I could hang out with friends all day before going home. The things that I find to be the most memorable of those seven years of my childhood are the things I have learned. I learned from the Boy Scouts the hard way that no matter how ridiculous or unnecessary it seems, listening to your parents is always the best path to follow. One winter campout, against my mother's advice, I refused to bring a jacket. That night at camp, the temperature dropped to fifteen degrees Farenheit, and I got frostbite. Needless to say, every winter campout after that, the first thing I packed was a jacket. Many of the lessons and ideas I learned as a kid have become what define my actions and words, today.

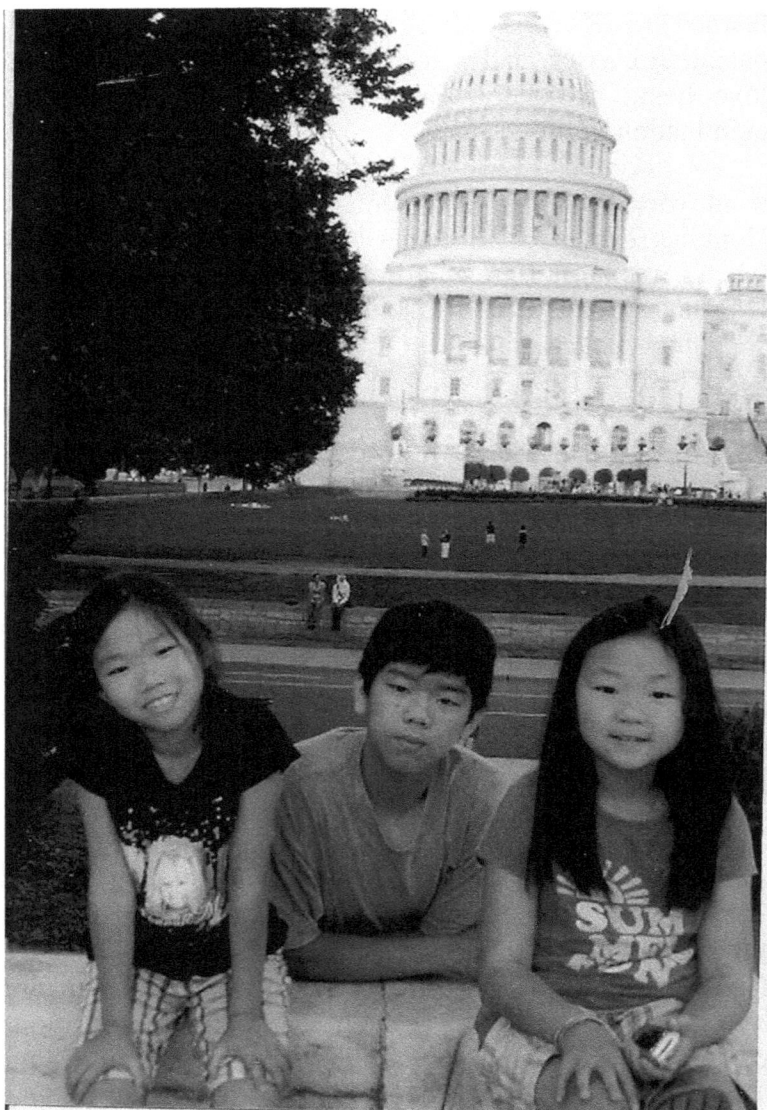

Then in fifth grade, against my furious protests, my parents forced my sisters and me to move to a new town, which was ironically called Newtown. Born and raised in Korea, my parents moved to America to pursue their dreams. Here they took up the dry cleaning profession after working for several years in the Bronx. Moving to Connecticut when I was 3, they bought a dry cleaning business in Bethel, called Pride Cleaners. I hold many fond memories of amusing myself on the rug floor in the front of that store, playing with blocks while my parents worked. The dry cleaning businesses my parents ran have always been a close part of my life. Ever since I was little, I was always at the store on weekends so my parents could look after me while I worked. I usually hated being there because there was nothing for me to do. I amused myself any way I could and liked playing with other kids. I remember Oliver, the child of the woman who owned the printing and laminating store behind the cleaners and Chris, the kid of the chef of the Italian restaurant, called Armando's, right next door. I remember running across the street to buy slurpees from Seven Eleven, and getting free bread from Armando's. Nowadays, I often help around at the store.

The dry cleaners are also a symbol of the American dream for my parents. They immigrated from Korea over 14 years ago with nothing but what they brought with them on the plane, but slowly and surely they have improved themselves in society so they could raise me and my two sisters to become successful in life. My parents work twelve hour days six days a week, so that they have enough cash to support the endeavors of their children. As they grew more successful my parents bought a larger store, and were able to support us even more. To give me a great education and to give my sisters a chance, they toil in the blazing heat of summer and the deep cold of winter to afford my tuition and to allow our family to live comfortably. My parents are one of the main reasons I try to work hard. I am deeply grateful to them for everything they have done for me.

My mother and father are role models for me. My mother is constantly working and never complains about how hard it is on her. Sometimes, when I am up late reading or doing schoolwork, I will go downstairs and see my mom still tailoring some article of clothing even though it is 1 AM. She sits in the cleaners and works without cease. Instead of hiring other people to work, she does the work of three different people to save money to use on my siblings and me. My father, on the other hand, wakes up early in the morning to get to work and to open the store. He is always the first to leave our house in the morning and the last to come back at night. My father, like my mom, is always working or helping me or my sisters. He drives us from place to place without complaint, even when I ask him to drive me home after a late party on Saturday night. My dad is always there for us, and he is one of the most reliable people I know. I don't really know much about my parents and their lives. I do know that they have sacrificed much and worked hard for me and my two sisters to be successful.

On April 11, 1998, Gemma, the older of my two little sisters, was born. Currently in sixth grade, she makes everything she does perfect. No matter how long it takes she will make sure that there are no errors or problems with whatever she is doing. Gemma spends hours on homework I would spend half an hour on, and practices sports and music relentlessly. When she practices violin, she plays for three hours, not because of necessity, but because she wants her playing to be perfect. As a result, even though she is fairly new, having only played for a year and a half, she is the best violinist in her school orchestra. She also figure skates, waking up at 5AM on school day so she can go to the rink and practice before school. Gemma relentlessly works to make everything she does successful. Even though she is not the smartest or most talented in her class, Gemma overcomes these barriers by sheer effort. In short, she is a perfectionist.

Catharina, or Cathy as we call her, was born a day before Gemma on April 10, 2000. She is an outgoing kid who loves to make friends and talk. She is well liked in school and loves to play tennis and soccer. Cathy seems to be very popular with her friends. Whenever we see a school friend outside of school, they always never hesitate to say hi to her and talk. She is very smart and picks up new thing quickly. I can teach her some pre-algebra level ideas and soon she is able to solve equations. Together, my two sisters get along well. Even though I'm not that great of an older brother, my two little sisters can have fun and enjoy themselves.

When my parents were successful enough in their first business, they had thoughts about expanding. This is where the conflict about moving arose. The new and much larger business, called Newtown Cleaners. they had bought, was in Newtown. I loved Brookfield, the town I lived in and had no desire to move. When I was told that I was going to not only have to switch schools, but actually move, I threw tantrums. What I didn't see was that this was the chance for my parents to move forward. This new business sort of symbolized the fruition of their dreams. Here, they could realize their goals of supporting their children to be successful in the future. I only hope that I can meet up to their expectations.

In Newtown, I enrolled in a parochial school, called St. Rose. I believe that my three years in this school affected my future the most. As with any middle school kid that had just transferred schools, I was nervous about making new friends. Luckily that wasn't a problem because I was able to quickly assimilate into my class. With Kevin, Jack, Johnny, Matt, and Nick, I shouldered what we believed was an overly strict educational system by trying to bypass all the rules, especially in science class, where Mrs. Dimon, a great, yet strict teacher, was constantly yelling at one of us to stop fooling around. By the end of eighth grade, we resorted "discreetly" to throwing these small rubber dinosaur toys that she kept in her classroom.

The St. Rose of Lima school is a parochial school in Newtown, CT, where the only Catholic Church in town runs one of the most successful schools in the state. Led by Monsignor Weiss, a well-loved priest, and run by Ms. Mary Maloney, a respected principal, the school is run to give its students a high level of education. As a result, the school won a Blue Ribbon award in 2009, which makes it officially one of the top middle schools in the state of Connecticut. Even though I had originally had hated the thought of even being in a Catholic school, in the end I feel blessed to have been able to enjoy my middle school education there.

At St. Rose, I discovered many things, but predominantly discovered my faith. Until then, I had just gone to church every Sunday, without really contemplating what it meant. I had attended a Korean Catholic Church in Hartsdale, NY, but it was more of a symbol of Korean ideals rather than one that inculcated the religion. I had gone to church more because I wanted to hang out with my Korean friends, rather than because I wanted to hang out with God. But when my life suddenly became filled with religion, I embraced it wholeheartedly. At this school, there was a way for me to truly identify myself through God. A few days before my eighth grade started, my school had a youth seminar, called Fan the Fire. For a day, I was able to talk to God, feeling his presence like I never had before. I emerged from the three hour adoration with a better knowledge of myself. Kneeling on grass under a large tent along with countless other youths from the tri-state area, we worshipped Jesus. By reflecting about who I was in the presence of God and asking him to help me find a path, I was beginning to figure out my identity. Spurred by the intense feelings of self-renewal and surrounded by thousands of other teens just like me, who had faith and complete trust in God, I too wanted to join this movement that somehow was able to let so many renew themselves. During that retreat, my faith grew along with my confidence in myself.

During middle school, I faced a crisis. I guess people would call it an identity crisis, because I couldn't tell anyone anything about myself. When asked to write down five things that I liked and disliked about myself in the religion class, I struggled to write down a single thing. I didn't really know who I was and wanted to understand more about myself and who I would become in the future.

This crisis was catalyzed by my trip to Korea during the summer of my seventh grade.

As it was the first time I returned to the land of my roots, my two month long trip to Korea filled the hole that had always been in my life. But the trip also created several more holes at the same time. I had been extremely excited about this trip because I would be able to fill a gap in my life. Ever since I can remember, all of my friends always met relatives during vacations, had fun with cousins, and visited grandparents in Florida. Unlike them, I had nobody to visit in America. So I always felt left out because I had never met any of my extended family members as my peers did. I had never known my aunts, uncles, cousins, and even grandparents. In fact, I was jealous of them because they could have what I saw as a complete life. In Korea, not only did I meet most of my family, but I was also even able to attend a Korean school for a month. I came back to America with a strong sense of Korean pride and a newfound racial identity. But, on the other hand, I didn't know whether I was Korean or American, I felt that I had to choose one and exclude the other. Was I a Korean living in America or was I an American, born Korean?

The flight to Korea was maybe the scariest twelve hours of my life. Never having seen my extended family before, I was anxious to meet them. I wondered if they would be nice or distant. I didn't know what to expect and became nervous. I tried to calm myself by watching some comedies on the TV in front of my chair, but it didn't seem to work. As soon as I got off the plane and met my aunts, uncles and cousins, I relaxed. They were nice people who were excited to see us. The next two months seemed to flash by in a blur. I had left school three weeks early for my trip to Korea, but to my dismay, my mother sent me to a school in Korea. So I left school early in America to go to school in Korea for a month longer than I was supposed to go.

At the time, all I could think about was the fact that my parents were forcing me to go to school during summer vacation, but as I look back now, it was a gratifying experience. It was actually pretty cool to be able to go to a Korean school versus the American one. The educational system and ideas are completely different from those in the US. In Korea, much more stress is placed on your test scores because ultimately, those are the ones that affect your final grade the most.

It was phenomenal living for two months with family I had never known before. Every weekend, we went on sightseeing trips all over Korea. I went to a Buddhist temple, the home of Yi Sun Shin, and amusement parks. Together with my family we watched the 2006 World Cup, and grew closer together. That trip to Korea indeed filled a hole in my life. When I came back, I had a renewed sense of national and family pride, but also, I had a bittersweet feeling. Because I knew it would be a long time before I ever saw them again.

This racial crisis led to me trying to rethink who I truly was. I thought about what I enjoyed, what I was skilled at, and my dreams for the future. The result of this inner probing was that I was nothing. I couldn't specify anything about myself. I could say that I was smart and good at math, but I really wasn't. I didn't truly enjoy playing tennis or the piano. I did not really like who I was. I hated being the only Asian in my class because I didn't want to be different. But this questioning of self drove me to try to uncover who I was. From sixth through eighth grade, I tried to separate myself from the rest of my class. It was not a physical separation, but a mental one. I realized that to understand who I was, I needed to be an individual instead of being part of the pack. In life, there really isn't much that one can call one's own. A lot that we all have as our own is in fact not our own. Until I could find what I had for myself, I couldn't call myself a person.

One of the things that I found that I truly enjoyed was science. It was a subject that I could put everything into and yet still have questions about. The science experience I gained at St. Rose was enormous, thanks to the teachings of Mrs. Dimon. Looking back, I understand that my dream of becoming a neurobiologist was really shaped during those three years in that classroom. Even though at the time, I hated having to write notes and listening to lectures on fossils, that knowledge stuck to me and created a deep seated love for biology. In eighth grade, I won first place at the Science Horizons science fair. My experiment was one that tested how well different types of water filtration methods worked on sea water and fresh water. I thought that this knowledge could help people find the most efficient filtration system for their water. I tested various water filtration methods by filtering seawater and freshwater. By testing for the contaminants, I could record how effective each system of filtration was. I recall once during my experimental process, I drank out of a water bottle that I had filled with seawater. Now, whenever I do an experiment, I label everything.

At St. Rose I started to look at a future that wasn't just the normal path in life. Because many of my friends wanted to go to private high school institutions, I, who had always assumed that I would be going to a normal public high school, also started to look at private schools. But instead of schools like Fairfield Prep, Immaculate High, and St. Joseph's that my friends all applied to, I wanted to get away from home. I hoped to apply to some boarding school so I could be more in charge of my own life and also so I could challenge myself. Could I excel without any parental support in a new environment where I spent all my time? I wanted the answer to this question even before I went to college. So I searched for schools, and in this search, my parents recommended some school I had never heard of before, called Hopkins. Apparently they had fallen in love with this school because it was a day school that was close to home, a prestigious academic institute, and probably most importantly, had been the school a prominent Korean named Harold Koh had attended. I had wanted to go off to some boarding school where I could be

independent of my family, but Hopkins was a simple day school, even though one of the greatest in Connecticut. The ironic thing is that the one school that I absolutely did not want to go to was Hopkins. And yet, in the end, I ended up applying to Hop, and I am extremely thankful for it. I believe that has been one of the best decisions in my life.

That first year at Hopkins was one full of new discoveries. A new experience in a challenging school was one I had looked forward to, but this school gave me more than I could handle. I started playing football and lacrosse for the first time and also joined many different clubs. The classes were all intense and exciting because I would always learn something else – something that I had never thought about. Discussions in English and History enlightened my mind towards new ideas about why different things occurred, and new revelations in Math and Biology deepened my love of those subjects. But the Hopkins experience is one that is deeper than just classes and discussions. I feel that the true depth of the school is expressed in what happens outside the classroom and afterschool. The highlights of my freshman year aren't from any great classes, or after school dances. They stem from the free periods or lunches, when my friends and I lounge on couches in Upper Heath or study together, filling out last minute homework assignments in the library study rooms. I have gained more from the talks, the laughs, the tribulations I have had with friends while sitting at a table or in the hallways than I can ever describe.

Going to Hopkins instead of some boarding school is maybe the best decision I have made. I believe that if I had gone to a boarding school like I had wanted, I would have failed miserably and ended up dropping out. I was not ready to survive by myself and couldn't be trusted to do so. Looking back, I now have gained much more self-control, self-organization, and self-sufficiency than I had back in eighth grade.

I have learned how to overcome the mental barrier that tells you that you can't do something. Before Hopkins football, before having to write 12 page term papers, before the long hours of hard studying, before Hopkins, I had no idea about the mental fortitude I needed to survive. Thanks to everything that I have experienced in my life and in my high school, I have learned how to overcome the mental barrier. And with that realization comes the fact that I have missed many opportunities in my life. I have come to see that these lost opportunities aren't something to regret and mourn over. They are there so I don't make the same mistakes again. So I move on into my future, wherever it takes me, and I know that I can overcome any obstacle steps in my path.

"Two Worlds"
Julie Oh

I dedicate my autobiography to students who might/might not go back to Korea during their high school years.

To start off, let me briefly explain to you my family background. I have a family of four, including my dad, Sang Hoon Oh, my mom, Sun Hee Lee, my sister, Eli Oh, and myself, Julie Oh. I was born and raised up in Mok-Dong in Seoul, Korea and lived there for 12 years of my life. I had been living a normal, plain life until my dad was assigned to work in the USA. Hearing the shocking news, my family hastily started to pack and prepared to live in the "dream country", America. So on March 23, 2005, my family finally arrived at the JFK airport with excitement and anticipation to start a new life in a country that we have only dreamed of. My dream was about to become real.

My dad, a few months later, told us the real reason why he decided to come to America despite the difficulty of speaking a foreign language. The reason was education. He had decided to come to America because of Eli and my education. My dad wanted us to have an opportunity to have various academic and social experiences in America. My dad, now that he has served five years here in America,

has to go back to Korea at any moment. I, only a little more than a year away from college, do not know whether I should prepare for Korean colleges or for American colleges because the colleges in two different countries have two different requirements for who they accept.

Let us go back to 2008, a year that I entered high school, and that is where I will begin my story.

High school is one of the most important times of one's life because how one performs academically and what he accomplishes during the time will determine which college he gets accepted to. It is not an exaggeration to say that one's future depends much on the achievements in high school. Although the importance of high school in Korea and America is similar, the requirements for the high school education are completely different in both countries. For those in my situation, who have the possibility of going back to Korea, must prepare themselves for both cases; staying in America and going back to their native country.

American colleges emphasize the importance of the SAT, GPA, grades one gets in his high school, the interview, and extracurricular programs one might have done during his high school years. However, in Korea, colleges emphasize their own entrance test and type of problems, especially math problems that have all the twists and turns (Korea is known for their extremely difficult math problems).

As a result of coming to the USA at the end of 5th grade, my Korean grammar, speaking, and writing are incomplete and underdeveloped, and unfortunately my English is even worse. Therefore, it has taken much more time for me to learn and even get good grades. However, I have tried my best and I will share my story with you.

To prepare myself for Korean colleges, I have done numerous things. First, I had been going to a Korean School called "Woo-Ri Korean School" every Saturday. The main objective of the school is to prepare the children of so-called "Ju Jae Won 주재원(businessman who was assigned to a foreign country to work but who would have to go back after a certain amount of time)" for the entrance exam they need to take to get accepted to Korean colleges when they go back to Korea. The school offers chances for students to learn the exact materials that the students in Korea learn. It offers subjects such as math, science, history, and literature for the upper grades and art, music, and gym on top of the main four subjects for the lower grades. I have very fond memories during the times I went to the school.

For example, I won an "Woo-Soo 우수" award (meaning "excellent") on the English to Korean and Korean to English translating competition that the school offered in 2009. My happiness doubled when I found out that I had received the top award in my class. In addition, I will always remember the fond memories I shared with my new friends and the teachers who taught students with passion and hope that the students will all get into their dream colleges.

However, it was not easy for me to attend the Korean School because of my busy schedule during the week, and it required my sacrifice and full commitment. My frustration began on the very first day. The school started at 9 AM and ended at 3 PM, every Saturday. This was very frustrating because I had to wake up at 8 in the morning to catch the bus and stay in the bus for almost an hour until we arrived at the school. The same applied when the school ended at 3; I had to go on the bus and wait an hour to get back home. The two hours seemed to be a huge waste of my time. Just from the first day of Korean School I was tired of the bus ride and began to think of going to Korean school as a waste of my time.

In addition to the bus ride, I dreaded Saturdays because it was so hard for me to complete homework and to study for exams when I had regular American high school Monday to Friday. Since I had entered the high school, the homework I faced was an incredible amount, up to a point I cried on some nights just because of the homework and the study load. But Korean School on top of the enormous high school work load I already had? The idea of going to Korea School seemed ridiculous.

However, now that I look back to those days, I am glad I had not stopped from going to the school. If I had stopped going there, I would not have met the teachers and my new friends I made there. But most importantly, I would not have had the chance to experience how students

in Korea study and by doing so I realized that I have to prepare for my future. Without going to the school I would not have had the valuable experience. The experience was an alarm, a wake-up call, for me to start planning for my uncertain future.

Aside from my regular high school work and Korean school work, I continued to solve Korean math problems. Now, you might wonder why I separate "Korean math" and "American math". I will briefly explain how those two differ. So-called "American math" tends to focus on basics whereas "Korean math" has twists and turns in the problems. This is evident in math classes in high schools.

In Korea, students go to academies, known as hak-won 학원. The private academies help students to excel in their school courses. Math academies are most common in Korea and students often go to the academies to fully understand what they have learned in their math classes. The academies distribute numerous math workbooks to help students practice numerous difficult problems that might appear on their tests. Getting help from academies begin from a very early age, often in elementary school. Nowadays, students' pace of learning has quickened, and students usually learn math that they will learn three years later. Since Korea has a very high mathematics standard and expects students to be able to solve difficult problems that have twists and turns, math in Korea, no matter what grade level, tends to be more difficult than it is in America. Therefore, for the Ju-Jae-Won students in foreign countries, it is crucial to maintain the pace with the students in Korea.

Truthfully, I am not very confident in math so it was essential for me to continue doing Korean math on my own, aside from any other work. This was not easy. I made a schedule and planned to finish a chapter in a workbook, every day. Although it was not easy to keep up with my separate study, I was able to do a little by little, each day. When I look back, although keeping up with students in Korea seemed ridiculous and impossible, I am glad I was able at least to try to reach the goal and actually accomplished a part of it. I just hope that if I have to go

back to Korea and prepare for Korean colleges, my desperate attempt to keep up will help me.

I have also done numerous activities to prepare for American colleges. First, I have done many volunteer works. I worked in the public library on school days, helping the librarians with organizing books in the right order, sending books, magazines, DVD's, and CD's to other libraries, and helping them to keep the library clean to provide a comfortable environment for readers. I worked at a geriatric center, helping elders eat, dress, walk, and exercise during the summer. In addition, I tutored 3rd graders, 4th graders, and 5th graders with their school work and exams. I was involved in many extracurricular programs. I participated in a musical called *Into the Woods* in 2009 at my high school. Since I enjoy singing, rehearsals that went on for 6 hours after school until 9 PM were never tiring. I enjoyed the musical very much and enjoyed every moment of it on the stage. In addition, I got into the JV tennis after a tryout. I was overjoyed when my coach, Mr. Streinsky, selected me as a one of the players. It was one of the happiest moments of my high school year. I also joined the winter track. I have done track for two years in middle school and my urge to run still remained as a part of me. I enjoyed the accomplished feeling I got after I ran miles.

Also, one of my biggest accomplishments of my high school sophomore year was being selected in the Bergen County Chorus. I was fortunate enough to sing with the best singers in the county and had so much fun. I was also very excited when the sophomore choir received the 1st place award, "Superior" award, in the Dorney Park singing competition and a 2nd place award, "Excellent" award, in a competition held in Philadelphia.

Aside from outside accomplishments, I am actively involved in many school clubs such as Hand-in-Hand (helping handicapped people), the Japanese Club, and the Chinese Club and plan to participate in National Honor Society in my junior year. Although there is a possibility of my going to a Korean college, there is a chance that I

may go to an American college. I sincerely hope that these accomplishments will help me when I apply for American colleges.

I do not want to limit myself to one category; I love experiencing many different kinds of activities and will continue to do so for the rest of my high school year!

Some people tell me to concentrate on school work and others tell me to start preparing for Korean colleges. Since my dad does not know when he will be assigned to go back to Korea, there has been many times when I inquired of myself, *Am I going in the right direction?* I am always anxious and worried about my future. However, there really is no right answer. The only way to know the answer is to experience it. But until then, I will do my best for what I can, getting good GPA's, participating in activities, doing volunteering works, and continuing to solve Korean math problems to keep up with the students in Korea. I want to advise those who are struggling to find the right answer, to find the right path to choose... if you do your best in what you can right now, there will be good results. Doing best right now will ensure the bright future. So keep doing your best!

"It All Started…"
James (Dong-Hwi) Kim

It all started since the time I placed my foot on JFK international airport on May 1st of 2000. Stepping out from the havoc of going through all the security, I stepped out into a cool night breeze, not knowing where I was, not knowing what lay ahead of me.

I was born on April 4th, 1993, in Suwon, South Korea. Upon my birth, I was given the name of Dong-Hwi Kim (김동휘), which means "Brightness from the East". Being the first grandson on my mother's side and the first son of the youngest child on my dad's side, I grew up with all the attention and love I could ever need. Growing up like this, in other words, I was spoiled; therefore, I grew up not knowing any hardships or any economic stress, as I would practically have anything I want.

I was also born into a religious family, as my dad was a pastor who was finishing his master's degree in theology, while my dad's brother was already a well-known pastor in Korea. My father's name was Sungmin Kim, while my mother's name was Eunmi Kim. My parents and I used to live at my grandmother's house in Namchang-dong, Suwon. One of the most prominent things I remember about living there was that, in order to get water to drink, we would go to a park behind our house to get water from a natural spring. But in order to go to the spring, we had to pass through a Buddhist temple with a huge Buddha statue. I don't know why but I hated that statue – probably due to the fact that I probably was raised in a Christian family. Other than that, most of my memories of Korea remain as nostalgic ones.

Then, one day, my father announced that we would be moving to the United States. But at the time I was too young to comprehend what the meaning of it really was. Before we left for the States, my family including my grandparents, uncles and aunts, went on a trip to a resort. Looking back, I now realize that the trip was a farewell goodbye between our families. During our stay at the resort, my whole family went to a bowling alley in the resort. For me, I was too young to bowl; therefore, I just wanted to go to an arcade right next door. But when I went to the arcade with my younger brother, I was missing the most crucial thing for an enjoyable time at the arcade; namely, money. When I went to my dad to ask him for money, he took me to the

hallway and asked me "Have fun here, but promise me that when you go to America that you won't play any games but study hard." All that came in to my ear was the first three words of the

sentence and the rest came to me as gibberish or something that I should just agree to in order to get my money. The days after that went by quickly or my memory just fails to recall anything after that "conversation" with my dad.

The day of our departure arrived, but remains as a blur to me up until the part where we were on the plane. I remember that it was my mom's birthday on the plane; therefore, we would celebrate May 1st as a combination of her birthday and our anniversary in the US. When we first arrived in the US, we located ourselves in the same town as the friend of my father, who convinced my dad to come. The place where we lived was Woodside, NY. For me, the place was an opposite of how I used to live. Looking back, the place we lived in was an apartment with just one bedroom and one bathroom, and what was horrible was that the apartment was literally rat-infested. Seeing this as a place where a pregnant woman, whose baby was due in a month, should not live, my dad moved into a brand new house in Flushing, NY. It was this place in Flushing, NY, where my mother had her baby, my little sister Sharon, and it was where I started my first year in the US school system.

The school I attended was P.S. 24. When my parents were registering me for the grade I should have been in at the time, which was second grade, the school board refused to put me into the second grade as I had not attended 1st grade in South Korea. What they did not realize was that the period and time in which school started in South Korea, was different from that of the US. In South Korea, schools start in March, while the

schools in the US start in September.
Due to the fact that I was leaving for US at the end of April, my parents decided not to send me to school in Korea because I would only go for a period of 2 months. Therefore when I tried to apply for the second grade in September, they refused as the record did not indicate that I had attended first grade. Thus, I was placed into the first grade.

For me, being placed into a level or a year younger than I was supposed to be was something of a disgrace or embarrassment. This irritated me greatly, as I would be with kids that were younger than me. Therefore, I tried to do my best with the American language that I would have to get accustomed with in order to be in the top of the class. What motivated me even further to quickly learn the language was that there was another Korean student (Whose name I forget) that was in the same class as me. This student, although being the same ethnicity but being born in the US, infuriated me intentionally by kicking at my desk or taking something that was mine as he knew that I could not tell on him or say anything to the teacher because I was new to the language.

Coping with this stress, I tried to excel in everything else other than English or Reading that was common throughout every country, such as math or art. One day, my teacher, Mrs. Paterson, came up to me while everyone was watching a movie and gave me a sheet of paper with words on it that I was not able to fully understand. So I asked the Korean student what it was, and he replied by saying that it was something that kids who could not speak English received. Upon hearing this, I was disheartened, thinking to myself that there was only so far I could go in a course of the year. As I did every day since I started school, I got picked up by my dad, along with other kids, as he worked a part time job as a driver. In between the times he picked them up and dropped them back off, we would go to the nearby library. When I gave my dad the sheet my teacher had given me, he asked me what it was, and I repeated what the Korean kid had told me. But my dad, apparently knowing a bit more English than I, thought that somehow it was something else. He went up to a librarian and asked what it was and came back and started typing into his translator to find out what it meant. After 5 minutes of strenuous work, he found out that the sheet of paper was not something that ESL students received, but it was actually a Principal's Award. Finding this out, I began to believe again that maybe it was possible for me to achieve something even at this stage.

Then second grade started. This year I was even more confident that I could do better. I realized what kind of person that Korean kid really was when I saw him in the hallway, as he told me that apparently his mom told him to stop talking Korean to me. I knew that it was his way of annoying me as he probably thought I was in the same state or level as last year. But I proved him wrong as I excelled in every one of my subjects and never missed any awards my school offered, from principal's awards to reading awards. But two months into what I thought would be a successful year, my father decided to move to a new place,

Connecticut. We moved to Bridgeport, Connecticut, and everything changed once again, and new challenges awaited me.

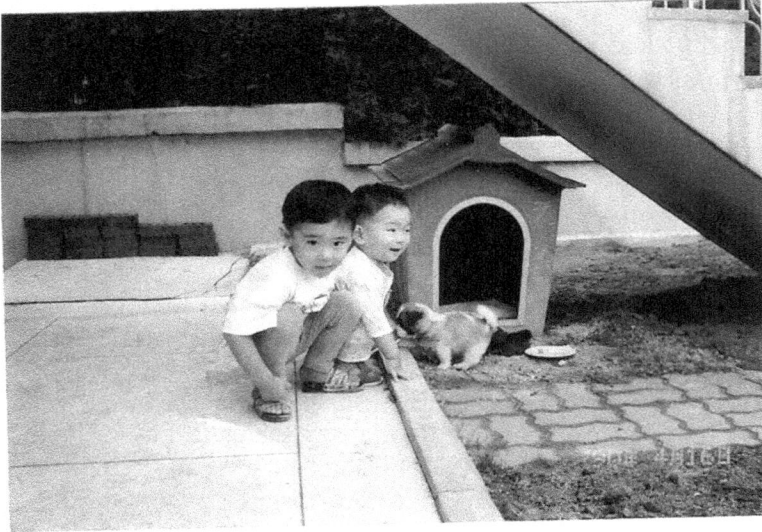

One of the factors that effected my dad's decision on moving to Bridgeport, CT, was the cost of the houses and the nearby magnet school, which he hoped I would be able to attend. But the public school (Edison School) I had to attend before I was accepted to the magnet schools was horrific. The situation even became worse when the school I was supposed to attend was full, and they transferred me to a public school in downtown Bridgeport. I can honestly say that the public school I was transferred to was even worse, as it was located in the area poorer than where I resided. But out of this situation, I was able to find something to be thankful for. One was that since the level of the school was below the level of the school I had attended in New York, I was able to take a test that enabled me to skip the 2nd grade and move on to the 3rd grade. Now, I was finally able to be with peers of my own age. By the end of the half of the school year, a room was opened in Edison School and I was able to transfer back.

Then, by the start of 4th grade I was accepted into the multicultural magnet school in Bridgeport, CT. My year at the magnet school was in a way, my chance to spread my wings, as I scored 5's on math and writing and 4 on reading on the CMT (Connecticut Mastery Test), placing me at the masters level. By the end of 4th grade, I was able to receive the Presidential Award for academic achievement. But while I started to adjust and perform well, my father decided to move again, partly because my little brother was unable to get into the magnet school and was stuck at the public schools. Therefore my father moved to Seymour, CT, a place where the academic level was higher and therefore better.

My time at Seymour was by far the most influential out of all the places I have lived. Seymour was very influential, as for the first time, I was able to attend a school for more than a year. My 5th grade in Seymour was nostalgic, as I met the teacher who has influenced me in many ways to become better. The teacher was Mrs. Eckhardt. She has influenced me greatly, in part, by encouraging me to do many things and by giving me the opportunities that I would not have had. But most importantly, she believed in me. An example of her efforts was her trying to get me into a program called Gemini (which was for 5th graders who have mastered the CMT). With her help I was able to adjust in the new school system, and by doing so, I was able to once again receive the Presidential Award for Academic

Achievement.

Besides academics, Seymour has been a great deal in my life and was a place that shaped who I am, today, as having lived there for 3 years, I was able, for the first time, to make best friends that would last a life-time. These friends were individuals that were of the utmost importance to me as they were friends that I have made for the first time in my life that actually knew who I was and what kind of person I was. My friends, Billy Stimple, Aldo Gallucci, and Austen Roman, helped me in many ways as they were the kind of friends that were actually there when you needed help or those who encouraged you to move forward when all seemed lost. The four of us became very close during our years in Seymour Middle School, as we came to sit at the same lunch table. After that we almost naturally became best friends, as we found out more about each other.

Although I was personally best friends with Billy, as he and I just developed this bond that was almost inseparable, Aldo was like my twin in many ways. This was because he and I were at the same places without ourselves even knowing who the other person was (before we ever became friends). One occasion that we apparently had met without knowing each other was during an art and music awards banquet, where two kids were chosen from each elementary school for their artistic or musical abilities. Aldo told me he had been there as he was chosen for playing the saxophone, and I, too, was chosen by my school to receive the award for my musical talents in saxophone. Other than that, we also were at the same banquet for our Presidential Award for Academic Excellence, and when he showed me the group picture, I was surprised to see myself standing next to Aldo, without ever realizing who he was.

Other than Aldo, Austen became my close friend just through school, as we were in couple of the same classes, and came to know each other even better. But my time at Seymour only seemed too good to last, and I was right. At the end of 7th grade, my father announced that he was going to move to New City, NY, as he took over as a senior pastor at the Rockland Korean Presbyterian Church. This move probably was a move that have affected me the most, out of all my relocations as this move actually forced me to leave behind what I valued most and what I came to love. My father, amidst all this, told me an old Korean aphorism: "Like a frog in a pond". What this means is that the world was big and my time, experience, and what I learned at Seymour was nothing compared to what was out there. Therefore, he tried to list the pros of the move, saying that it would eventually help me in the future.

The church that my father was appointed to is called Rockland Korean Presbyterian Church. The Church, being located at 109 South Rt. 303, Congers, NY, is far enough that my family had to move. The church had chosen my father to become their senior pastor after a series of interviews and

listening to the sermons of my father.

I remember that on the day of his first sermon for the Rockland Korean Presbyterian Church to show how he was like, there was a heavy snowstorm, where the news forecast warned everyone to stay inside. My father trying to show his "determination", took us into the storm for a trip that lasted 3 hours; the drive should have lasted only a little bit more than an hour. I remember that I had to get out of the car and push the car out as it was stuck in a snow pile. I personally think that even though my father's sermons were good, it was this act that gave him points and that helped him to be picked as the senior pastor of Rockland Korean Presbyterian Church.

The history of the church is mostly unknown to me and my family. All I know is that (and I'm pretty sure I know almost as much as my father knows) the church is almost 10 years old, previous to our coming. Also, the reason they were in need of a new pastor was that the old pastor apparently got into some legal issues, as his father used the church to do illegal immigrant transactions. For these reasons, the church had split, and the old pastor was forced to resign. This troubled church was the place my father was appointed to. At first I did not even know in the slightest bit what was going on. But as my father did not know the church members very well, or whom to trust, he usually settled matters by himself, and as his English is limited, I was his translator. One example is when we received calls from the IRS (Internal Revenue Service); my father had me come along in order to translate the events that were going on, such as the missing tax reports from our church in the previous years we were not there. I, having to translate this for my father, became very aware and keen to the situation of our church and its predicaments. My father resolved this matter by registering our church as a whole new church, therefore having no relations to the activities of the past church or its troubles. When the issue was over, I thought that was the end of the troubles my father would face from the church, but I guess that was just the start.

Other than the Church, the move to New City, NY, like my father had said, was a completely new experience and a completely different environment. Like the old Korean saying, I realized that I became too accustomed to that one place, as I had thought that Seymour was all there was to it in the world – that it was like the rest of the world – but I was wrong. Being the valedictorian for the last 5 years in CT, I assumed that it would

be the same in NY. But I could not have been more wrong, as from the moment I stepped into the new school, which was called Felix V. Festa Middle School, one of the largest middle schools in NY, consisting of more than 2000 kids, the classes and the curriculum was rigorous and challenging, unlike the ones I was used to in CT. Also I did not realize how different a school system could be between two states.

In Clarkstown District that I was in, academic level was very high. As I was not familiar with the District's school system, I was placed into all regents classes, except for math. At first I did not know that students were separated into different classes according to their levels. As I found out that I was placed into regent classes which was the most basic class, and that there were honor classes and classes higher than that, I was immediately put under tremendous amount of stress, as all I could think about was how inferior I felt compared to others. Although I excelled at these regents classes, I knew that I was nothing compared to those of higher classes. From then on it became my goal to raise all of my classes to those of honors or higher levels with any means necessary. I did not know at the time if it was a good goal or not, but I was desperate, as I was the type that could not deal with the feeling of being inferior to fellow peers. Therefore, for the sophomore year, I raised all my classes to honors, and if the teachers did not recommend it, I got into the classes by filling out waivers. For me at the time, the teachers who did not recommend me even if I asked them were uncaring. I thought this because for me, I believed that the teachers did not know the situation I was in, the pressure I had on my shoulders, especially the ones from my father. At first I was basically studying not for myself, but because my father forced me to, and because only getting good grades made my father proud of me. Now, when I look back, I realize how far that kind of motivation can spur you, and trust me – it was not that far.

Then throughout my years at NY, I was able to attend many Christian retreats, and camps, that were unavailable to me at CT. Personally, these retreats and camps had no effect on me – that especially my father wanted, which was to experience the Holy Spirit. But the times at the retreats made me realize or actually understand what my father had said, that I was not trying to be someone rich or famous for my own benefit, but for a higher good. One retreat was by the name of Immanuel. This retreat was very well organized as it was not hosted by just one church, but by many churches that were part of the KAPC (Korean American Presbyterian Church) that our church was a part of, thanks to my father. My father said that if I was studying or doing anything else to become someone rich for myself, it would be just selfish. With these retreats, I came to set my goal for becoming wealthy not for personal gain, but for the glory of God. As my father would always tell me, "Who would have a higher influence? A common man or someone of a higher status, like the president?" Although I say that I have set my goal to

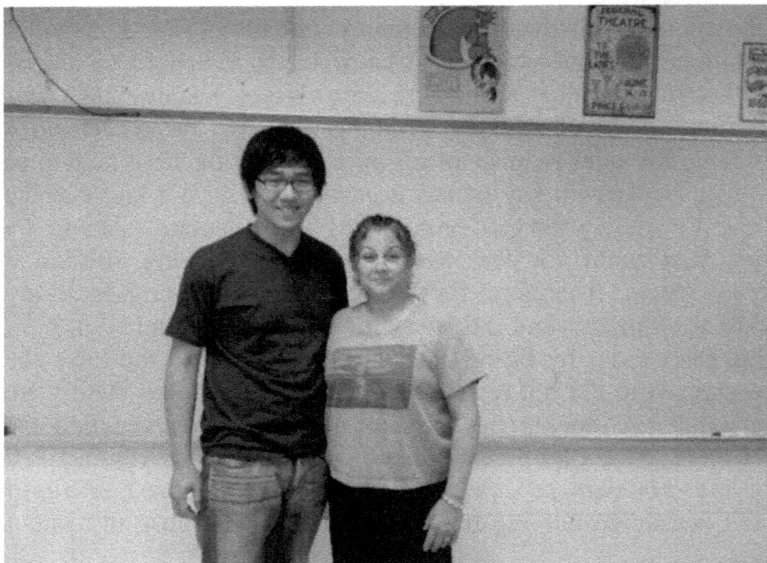

become a better person for the glory of God, I still struggle in fully believing what I myself claim to believe. But hopefully, by always saying that I would live for the glory of God, I would come to believe or come to a revelation.

Since the first day of my father's appointment as the senior pastor at Rockland Korean Presbyterian Church, it naturally became my duty to become the president of my youth group. At first, I accepted being the leader of the youth group, because my father needed help in organizing the disoriented church. But the church members placed a lot of pressure on me to take this position. The position I was in was very difficult, as there were only two options for me; one was becoming the youth group leader, and the other was to reject the position. What made these options pressure-packed was that if I had accepted, it wasn't seen as a good deed or a good decision, but instead it was seen as something that was my inevitable duty. I hated the treatment that was given to me by the church members, as I was a normal person just like them, being able to make my own decisions. But when I made decisions, such as volunteering to become the youth group leader or volunteering at church events, they saw it as natural acts that I had to dutifully do, although it was my decision and I made personal sacrifices to do it. I saw this more clearly when a kid that went to my church and I did the same thing, they would pour adulation on him on his commitment, while they would give me the cold shoulder. I partially understood their treatment, as this was the way people usually acted towards people of higher status or the children of these people (like senior pastors), and I was used to it. But what always got me, was when a group of kids and I got into some trouble, I would be the one that they would always blame. But as the oldest child, I tried my best to tolerate all these acts, as my father would tell me a Korean saying that literally translated to "Your face is my face," which means metaphorically that the actions or behaviors I commit reflects on my father, as he raised me, and his teachings would be the reasons for the way I would behave.

Although I came to know my status and acknowledge the treatment I would receive as long as I was the pastor's son, I was infuriated when I saw that my little sister was being harassed and bullied by the kids of her age; as kids of the pastor, we were rendered helpless. We were helpless because even if we did the slightest thing such as yell at a kid, swear at a kid, or

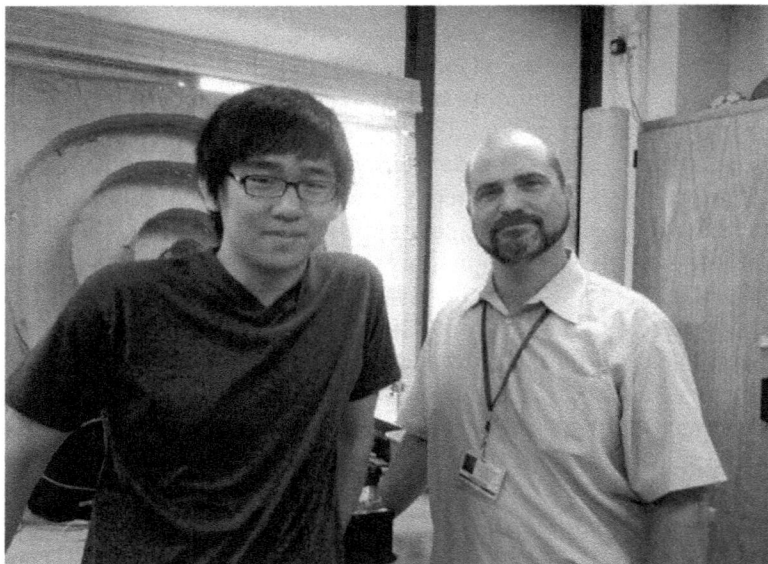

even hit a kid (who hit us), all the blame would be on us, indirectly affecting our father and the church. But even this was the case, for me I could not accept the fact that my little sister was being hurt, and no matter how screwed up the society's rules might be, what was wrong was wrong. I made my point clear by coming to my sister's side and scolding them, although they ran away to their parents crying (which I felt a jolt of fear for). I felt self-satisfaction for teaching those kids a lesson, although it was not even close to what I would have done if I was not the pastor's kid. After that, although there were few other incidents, the situation became better as, I guess God started alleviating the tensions. I saw this clearly as the people who disrupted the church and caused havoc, left the church on their own accords, and new but more faithful people replaced their spots.

Then I was able to make new friends at the new school. One of my best friends that I have made since I move to New City which was in Rockland County was Justin Pak. We had been friends since the 2nd day of my school at Felix V. Festa Middle School. Justin too had moved to New City this year and therefore did not know anyone just like me. The way in which we became friends was kind of childish and funny as we had 3 classes together and one of them happened to be our last period. As we waited for our buses, Justin came up to me and asked me if I was Korean. When I replied that I was, we became natural friends from then on. Justin was a very close friend to me, as he happened to be Korean and he had a personality which was very relaxing and funny, so in the past 3 years we have been friends, we have never gotten into any fights.

Then, in my freshman year came my other close friend, Derrick Kim. Derrick had come to the US that year in order to

101

play golf. At first I met him through a friend of mine, who asked me to become friends with him as he was new, so I just started off by saying "Hi" and stuff. But even before we knew it, we were close enough to be coming over each other's houses. These two are two of my most prominent friends, as they both are close enough to me that I was able to get them to go to my church.

This was a big deal for my part, as our church was just starting off; we were not settled down like other bigger churches that had praise teams or many kids. Therefore in order to ask a friend of mine to come to a church such as ours, we had to be very close. Do not get me wrong; I am not saying that our church is bad, but that it is just new. And trust me; it will get bigger and become a house of worship that is right in the eyes of God.

The thing that I thought was the sealing deal that marked how close our friendship was is that Justin came to my church, although he was a Catholic and his parents went to a Catholic church, and Derrick came to my church, although he was formerly a Buddhist and had recently converted, as his parents went to a different church. Starting to attend my church solely for the reason of being my friend allowed me to see that these were true friends. Of course, now I hope and pray that they are coming not for me but to learn more about God.

As our church became more settled in, I set a goal to expand our small youth group as much as possible. In order to achieve this goal, I recently started our praise team, in which I play the guitar, and I would lead our praise team, among other responsibilities, such as being the president of the youth group. I really pray and hope every day that eventually our youth group would grow. I can partly see the progress now although it might be slow; kids are starting to come.

Following my father's example, I am still trying to strengthen the faith and beliefs of the current kids that attend our youth group. It is not just them, but also I need the most strengthening and the help of God, if I want to even get close to accomplishing this goal. Therefore being part of the praise team and the youth group, I started to believe that whoever I became, I would do it in order to glorify God.

Another motivation for me, or something that actually made me feel grateful for what I had was volunteering at Milal (미랄선교단). Milal, translated to "The American Wheat Mission", had the objective of helping the disabled. In all honesty, I first volunteered in order to get some volunteer hours for college and for school. But since my first day, a pang of guilt hit me, as the kids that I volunteered with were so innocent and altruistic. Being with them made me realize how wrong it was of me to try and volunteer for self-benefit, while the whole concept of volunteering was to help others. When I started volunteering around February of 2009, the kid that I was assigned to had the name of Chris. Chris had autism and mental disabilities that disabled him from talking and kept him at the mental level of a 5 year old. Seeing someone at a condition like this firsthand and working with him, I realized how grateful I should be to God for giving me a healthy body and mind. After I realized this, my volunteer work at Milal was not for the hours but more for in the spirit of genuine service, as I felt it was necessary for me to do my part in helping others with the gifts that God had given me. From this, I came firmly to resolve that what I do in life will be for the glory of God, and what I become will also be for the glory of God.

While I was preoccupied with all the previous things, my junior year started. I had heard many rumors that junior year was the worst year in high school, and I came to realize that it actually was. The workload was incomparable to the other years in high school. Although the school work that I had to deal with such as AP U.S. History, AP Physics, or other classes was bearable, what made it the hardest year was the SAT's that we had to study for and take. On top of that, I had a part-time job at a coffee store, called Seattle's Best. The thing I was upset about was that I had to quit Varsity football in order to be able to study for all my tests and SAT's. I was upset because I had attended all the summer camps and sessions since last year in order to play for the upcoming season, but I had to quit right about when our season was actually about to start. If I did not quit, I would have played offensive tackle or guard, although I like defense better. But I realized that I had to make sacrifices to achieve my dream of becoming a leader to help people in the future. To become an effective leader, I knew that I had to go to a good college that would provide a good training for leadership.

Without football, my junior year started. When my first report card came out, it was disheartening as I received a C in AP US History; this was the first time I received anything lower than an A in a history class. Because of such a low grade, I was faced with the decision of whether or not I should drop it. But I decided to go all the way through with it. Then, on December I took my first SAT, and got a score of 1890 which I thought was okay for my first time as I had received 176 on my PSAT, which was supposedly easier. But for the second time I took the SAT which was on March; I took off almost all my work in order to study for it. But when I got back the score, I was surprised to find out that my score had dropped 100 points, from an 1890 to a 1790. For me, this result was almost unrealistic, as I had actually studied for this one and was prepared for it. While I was stressed as it was, I went further into despair as my father just stopped talking to me for like a week or two. This act by my father just upset me, as I expected some kind of encouragement or pity.

Although taking it for the third time seemed like my score would go down even more, what encouraged me to take it was a Korean Drama by the name of "God of Study". It was odd how I happened to see this drama, but what was stranger was how the drama fit my life; the similarities were too big to be a coincidence. Therefore, I believed that it was God's doing. What happened in the drama relates to me as the character in the drama, although stupid, studies day and night for a final, putting substantial amount of effort. But when he received his score back, it was even lower than the score he received without studying. When he was about to give up, the teacher in the drama encouraged him to take it again, as study was something that did not lie and did not go away – that countless effort will eventually pay off. Listening to the teacher, the student took it again, studying even harder than before and received almost a perfect score that allowed him to go to his dream college. This drama therefore motivated me to take it again on the June test of 2010, the last month of my junior year. But during my meeting with my guidance counselor to plan for colleges, she asked me what colleges I was looking at. Honestly, I did not want to say anything as my SAT scores was not even close enough to get me into the schools I wanted, such as Johns Hopkins or Cornell, as I wanted to become a medical doctor. When I replied that I did not look at colleges due to the fact that I did not receive the scores that I wanted, she asked me what score I was looking for on the SAT. When I said that about 650 on the Critical Reading section, she told me it was unlikely, and personally I didn't blame her, as I received a score of 580 on Critical Reading the first time and 520 the second time, and she only had my records to work with. Knowing this I decided not to argue further but to actually show her.

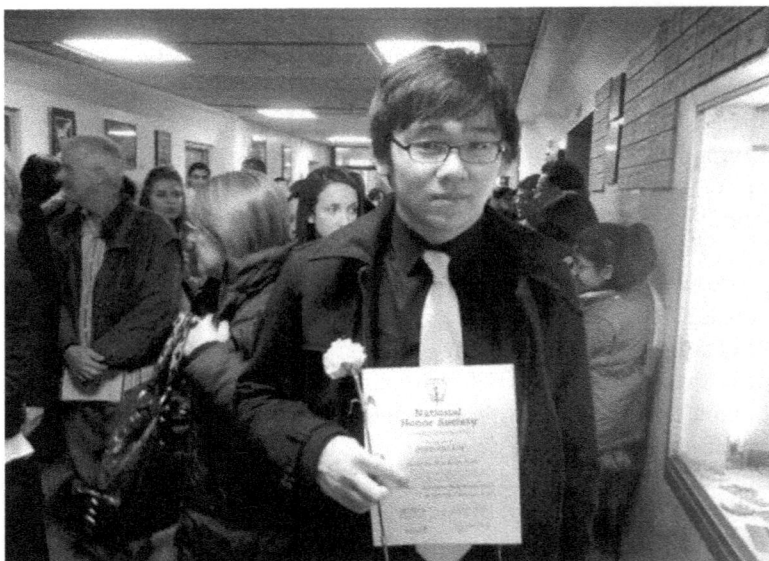

But trying to take the SAT in June was something that I had tried to avoid, as it meant that I would have to double up on my studying as I would have to study for my finals at the same time. But I guess somehow I managed to put up with it. Then, a week ago my SAT scores came back. I received a 2040, and with the math score from the first SAT, my super score was a 2100. And I received a perfect essay score of 12, this time, while on the previous two tests I was unable to get above a 10. What was particularly exciting was the fact that my Critical Reading score on the June 2010 SAT test was 690, which showed that I was able to break the 650. I had proven to my guidance counselor that I can achieve the goals that I set for myself, so I was very happy. It is good to good work to achieve beyond people's expectations. Also, I realized that it is important not to let past failures or weaknesses hinder me from striving for my dreams. Now, I am just waiting for my grades for the final I had taken last week, on the third week of June of 2010. Hopefully, I did well on all of my other tests as I did on English, as I received a 97% on the English final, as I was told by my teacher.

Although I am waiting for my results to come back, I just hope no matter how I do I will live for the glory of God. As I believe that God, will lead me in the right direction, and in believing this, I will continue to pursue my goal of becoming a world-renowned person as a doctor or whatever God leads me into becoming to glorify God's name and to praise God. This is what I feel and believe up to this stage of my life, where as of now, I am 17 and headed to my summer Christian retreat "Immanuel" for my second time at Nyack College. I hope that during the retreat I will come even closer to God and better understand his plans for me. Although I feel like I have learned a lot in the past 17 years of my life, I have a long way to go before even getting close to where I would like to be in relation to God and in relation to the achievements that I would like to make in my life in the field Medicine and helping those in need in whichever way that God wants me to.

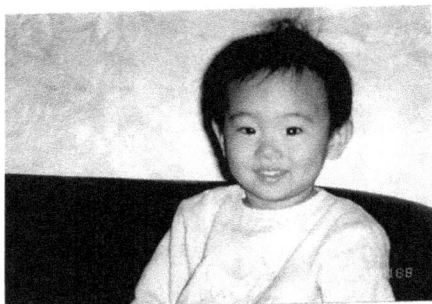

"Still Looking…"
Rei Fujino Park

The Beginning

In the depth of time, I slept. Not knowing who I was or where I was, I was but a ball of flesh, curled up with my legs and arms tucked in as if to protect myself from danger, trapped in this world. But suddenly, a sliver of light embraced me gently with its warmth and freed me from the abyss. I cried tears of mixed emotions. All I knew was that I was born and the hourglass began.

On a cold winter night, I was born in the Nowon-Gu hospital in Seoul, Korea, at 2:44 A.M on December 11, 1992. It was colder than usual that night, which made it difficult for my mom to get to the clinic. Through her efforts, I was born into this world. Although every person is "different," I am proud of being even more different. What sets me apart from all these "different" people is that my blood is a fusion of two different cultures, two rival countries. My dad is Korean, while my mom is Japanese. Yes, I was born from the love of two enemies.

There is a long history filled with war and hatred between the country of Korea and Japan. Fortunately, unlike Romeo and Juliet, there wasn't any romantic drama or tragedy between my parents. Although there were few disagreements amongst my grandparents, the strong and honest feelings of my parents towards one another broke that tense atmosphere and evolved it into that of harmony and love. The story of my dad, Jin Su Park, and my mom, Keiko Fuijino began on the day of their auspicious meeting.

The Enemy's Encounter

Who are you? Are you my enemy? What makes you an enemy, my enemy? People believe that enemies are individuals who have come to hate each other through their differences, actions, or maybe even jealousy; but are these really the pieces that create the existence of the term enemies? No? Yes? It really depends on how you see the term. But don't forget...enemies are also part of your life and are humans like yourselves. So, is it possible that enemies can come to understand each other, or maybe even love each other...?

The surname Park, which comes from the Korean word for "gourd," can be traced back into the Silla Dynasty (57 BC – 935 AD) when King Hyeokgeose Park ruled. When seven princes were born, one of their descendants became a farmer and a fisherman. Through this tree of ancestry, my grandfather, Bong Yeol Park was born. He lived in the countryside as a farmer and a fisherman with his brother, Yeong Gi Park. Afterwards, he met my grandmother, Seo In Duk, and gave birth to my father, Jin Su Park. Wanting his children to have a good education, my grandpa moved to a town near a small school. My dad would always tell me stories about his childhood, which I found amusing. Sometimes he tells me about how he would have to cross over mountains by foot for several hours to be able to get to and return from school. Other times, he would tell me about the lack of computers back in his day. Eventually, he graduated from Cheong Ju University, where he majored in Korean literature and joined the Korean Military.

Because he tried so hard, he was promoted into a special force of Commandos. This group specialized in completing many difficult trials that the regulars couldn't do, such as sabotage, survival, and scouting missions. His military life was a challenge. There was always heavy training daily- even under the blazing sun in the summer and the freezing cold in the winter. After several training sessions and missions, he trained himself to eat anything, even worms. Although military life was challenging for him, he enjoyed spending his time with his fellow comrades.

Then, there's the long history of the Fujino family, which unfortunately only has records that date from the Samurai Era. The majority of my Fujino ancestors worked as doctors for the Emperor of that time. My grandfather, Michio Fujino didn't become a doctor. Instead, he worked at a school. On the other hand, the Toyoshimas, my grandmother's ancestry, were full of business men and women. Some were successful,

while the others were not. My great, great grandfather was a successful man. He had a business of lending houses to his customers who brought him great income and a luxurious life. My grandmother, Itoe Fujino, as a little girl, was treated like a princess when she was young, until the great dilemma. My great grandfather, Isaburo Toyoshima, to whom the inheritance and business was passed down to, failed to continue the business. Through his mistake of buying the stock, everything was lost. Since, my grandmothers's mother, Toki Toyoshima left the world at an early age due to a disease and Isaburo couldn't take care of his two children, they were in a hopeless situation. As a result, he left them with his distant relatives. My grandmother and her brother lived together for a while, but they were eventually separated into different households. This wasn't the end of their misfortune.

Their new family wasn't warm and welcoming. My grandmother and her brother had to work hard for their shelter, food, and warmth. My grandmother's younger brother, Hideaki Toyoshima, who couldn't take his new family's cold rejection, ran away to Tokyo to start a new life. He wasn't successful. He was only able to become a taxi driver who received low income. My grandmother, who wasn't as badly treated as her brother, worked hard under her relatives to escape from their rules and

111

to live by her own. She didn't want to be indebted to them forever, so she studied hard to become a teacher. Her dream came true at an age of nineteen. Although she wished to see her brother, she couldn't reunite with him for more than 30 years when he died in 2008. My grandmother taught for 40 years, and during her career, she met my grandfather through *Omiai,* or meeting someone through one's colleagues.

Through them, my mom, Keiko Fujino and my uncle, Yousuke Fujino was born in Fukuoka City. My mom, who loved to read books and to learn history, joined the history club during her school year. After majoring in English and graduating from college, she worked in a real estate company. Unlike my mom, my uncle was a science and math major. He majored in physics and attended one of the best universities in Tokyo, the Tokyo Institute of Technology. He currently works in a glass company where he researches special types of glasses such as the computer screen and the car window shield. He is a very successful man.

Although my mom and dad lived different lives, they shared one thing in common; their religion. Their religion's mission is to unite religions, nation, and people's relationships. My mom and dad met through their church activities. They weren't the ones to choose their partner, but they were both

very happy with each other. They continued to participate in global peace activities and soon began to live their life together.

At first, my grandparents weren't confident with their decisions because Japan and Korea were still considered enemies that time. However, my parents both tried their best to convince my grandparents that they loved each other. My Japanese grandparents didn't mind as long as they were happy with their decision. Although it took longer to convince my Korean grandparents, through a lot of persuasion, they agreed. My mom worked especially hard to be acknowledged by trying to follow the Korean culture of eating spicy food which she wasn't used to eating. When my grandma gave her some *hwae-top-bab* to eat, she hesitated at first, but eventually ate an entire bowl. While eating, she tried so hard to hold in her tears. Because of them, my story begins.

The Girl Who Tells the Story

Once *upon a time, there was a girl with a twisted character that she herself couldn't comprehend. She was a confused one, not knowing how to accept life. She couldn't really understand herself or the world. She was just there... She often escaped reality and lived in her own world of fantasy. She jumped from world to world thinking that she has escaped, but little did she know that reality wasn't something one could escape easily from...*

As some of you may already know from the title of my autobiography, my name is Rei Fujino Park (meaning "polite" in Japanese). My Korean name is Ye Jong Park. I am seventeen years old and am currently attending Francis Lewis High School. I am living with my family of seven, which includes my cousin, Grace Park, who came to stay with us as a global transfer student. I have already introduced my parents, Jin Su Park and Keiko Fujino. Next, I would like to introduce my three siblings, but before I do, I would like to talk a little about myself.

If I were to describe myself, I would say that I am an average girl. I love to play sports outside and observe unique insects, while collecting cicada shells during the summer. Aside from my wild side, I tend to start drawing whenever I see paper and a writing utensil, and I love listening to music and playing instrument. I am currently learning how to play the violin at my school, and am also eager to learn the piano, guitar, drum, etc... I admire those who have the skill to play instruments, create beautiful tunes and melodies. It makes me smile and my blood rush with excitement. I also enjoy listening to the singers sing with their beat and lyrics. Music is like magic to me. I enter another world whenever music plays. Art also has the same effect on me. When I draw, I feel as though I am creating something and tracing my mind on the paper. I love to watch animations and find each and every one of its plots and characters fascinating. It drew me in because I later found out that it was something a little different from reality. One time, while watching *Dragonball Z* with my siblings, I tried to imitate Goku's special move; the kame-hame-ha. Although I had been very confident that an energy ball would burst out of my hands, I was disappointed to see that it didn't.

My family would call me "multi-faced" even to this day. The reason is the fact that I am a shy, quiet girl at school who changes into her true wild character at home. Although this is not so true now, in the past, there was a big gap in my personality. It's not the fact that I was polite to the elderly, eerily nice to my friends, a monster to my siblings, and a hyper maniac at night that defined me as multi-faced. I was a completely different person once I entered the outside world. Both my voice and my posture changed whenever I went outside. When I think back on it now, I think I was pretty skilled at changing my character. I was proud of the fact that I was able to suppress my true feelings because for some people it is a very hard thing to do. However, this was just a misunderstanding of my strength and weakness. One time, there was a girl who was pointed out at as annoying and dull in my class. I, who wasn't very popular at that time, couldn't help her because I was afraid to be in her place. Instead, I hid my true feeling in these matters and went along with my so-called "friends." The people who taunted and avoided her were despicable, but I myself, who couldn't

speak out my true thought and try to help her, was even lower.

After graduating middle school, I began to grow tired of smiling when I wasn't even happy, agreeing when I disagreed, and pretending to be an innocent girl while thinking evil thoughts in the back of my head. I would sometimes adjust myself to protect myself from any fingers pointing my way. I preferred to have a quiet school life.

At this point, some people may say that I am strange or unique. Others may find it to be normal, but my weird character doesn't end here.

Beyond the Mirror

When one becomes lost in a world, one tends to seek answers within one. In one's conscience lies another existence, an existence very close to us. When one reaches out for that existence, it reaches back. Look closer and it looks similar to us. Listen carefully and it whispers... "I am still asleep, but I will awaken once you grow aware of my existence...after all...I am you..."

Have you ever stared at a mirror and asked yourself, "Who am I?" I haven't. I just thought that it was a strange thing to do, since the answer seemed to be obvious. I was Rei, but was that all I was? I was a curious one. I don't remember how it began, but at one point in time I started to ask a lot of serious questions to myself. Who am I? Why was I born? What is my purpose? You could say that I had reached the stage where I began to take life seriously. I would ask my parents these questions, but they would just laugh and say, "You are Rei, our daughter. Your purpose is to live for God." That wasn't the answer that I wanted to hear from them. Their answers were too vague and normal. That was when something occurred to me. I heard a faint voice in the back of my head. I often tried to ignore it, but after a while, I came to accept it. When I did, I began to hear the voices clearly and saw her, the other me.

Strange as it was, it was also natural. She saved me from depressions and gave me the answers that I sought. She was also

the friend whom I could always share my thoughts and opinions with. She was an honest one. I would often get in trouble from my parents for assaulting my siblings. I would then be sent to a room to carry out my Asian punishment of having to raise both my arms over my head and to hold it there until I was told to put them down.

While I was in that painful positions, "She" would always come out and ask, "Why do you always attack your siblings?" and I would answer, "It's their fault." She would sigh and look at me as if I were a pitiful creature. Then, "She" would hit me on the head hard with her bare knuckles and lecture me. To clear up any confusions or before you think that I am insane; "She" doesn't have a physical form. She is like an imaginary friend, but with a much deeper connection. She was me, so if she hits me, it was like hitting myself. I believe that she was the one who understood me the best because I was taught from the true world of reality that no one can be trusted. However, my belief didn't agree with my gullible character. I am the type who would believe in one's word till the very end and even accept sweets from my enemy. On the contrary, trusting someone can also be strength. People would need great courage to actually put their faith in someone, and risking the result of betrayal. Sometimes, I was too cowardly to trust someone because I was afraid of its consequences.

Nightmare

Little girl, why do you fear? I am but a Nightmare that lives in your dreams. Run away and I shall follow you till you reach the end who calls itself Death...accept me and I shall be your strength...

In 2000, I moved to New York due to my father's business. Before moving to NY, I lived in Denmark, where I learned how to speak Danish and made many Danish friends. I had adapted to the environment there quite quickly and well, but in New York it was different. Not only was there a language barrier, but the students were also hard to get along with. I managed to survive 2nd grade without a problem, but 3rd grade was a challenge for me. On my third year, I transferred to a different elementary school called P.S 31. Truthfully, I hated this school. Well, at least my 1st year of school in it. The school itself wasn't bad, but I couldn't stand the students and the teachers who attended there, although my view changed after my first year. My first year in this school wasn't a memorable one.

During my first year as a 3rd grader there, my teacher, Ms. Uvar, partnered me up with a Korean girl named Susan as

my translator, since I didn't know any English back then. It went well until she started to get annoyed at translating every single thing for me. I didn't blame her, but at the same time, didn't expect myself to learn a whole new different language in just a couple of months. Therefore, I handled her sharp glares that sent jolts through my spine pretty well until two new "friends" joined in. The ironic part of this turnout was that I wasn't taunted by Americans, but by my own kind, Koreans. To make matters worse, the two others who joined in were ESL students like me. I never understood what separated me from those two. While this was going on, my teacher just pretended that we were all best friends. The problem was that she didn't see that I was not part of the three-musketeers. Ever since that horrible year of taunting, my relationship with Koreans wasn't that stable. Yet, ironically again, the first best friend that I made was Korean. That was when I thought to myself, "This world works in strange ways."

This event was one of the key triggers in my life that caused me to become the person that I am today. I become cautious when I come in contact with people and sensitive when it comes to other people's feelings. This was also what led to my other self whom I always consult with. In the past, making friends was like taming an animal. Once I gained their trust, I had to be careful not to lose them. I was afraid. I didn't want to feel the sensation of loneliness in the dark, where no one accepted me. If they couldn't acknowledge me for who I was, I decided that it was better for me to change myself into a person whom they can accept.

I used to think that it was easier to become friends with animals than people. One day, someone gave me two hamsters, and I became quite close to one of them. One of them, Indo, was a lazy, but a violent fellow. It would bite everyone in my family despite our innocent intentions in cleaning its cage. Although I tried to get close to it several times, it always rejected me. It just continued to ignore us by eating and growing fatter. It seemed to be enjoying itself so I decided to leave him be. The other one, Hamtaro was my favorite. I got its name from the TV show, *Hamtaro*. It was calmer and trusting than Indo. It even recognized me whenever I stuck my hand inside the cage. It would hop on top of my hand and nibble it. It would sometimes do its "business" on my hand, but I didn't mind. When it died, I was really upset. I was really sad when it died even though it lived a long life. I remember crying as I buried it under a flower bush and I would sometimes visit it and realized that easy friendship didn't last.

Friends

Relations require patience. Not everyone is perfect. Neither are their thoughts nor view. They may see things in a different way. But give them

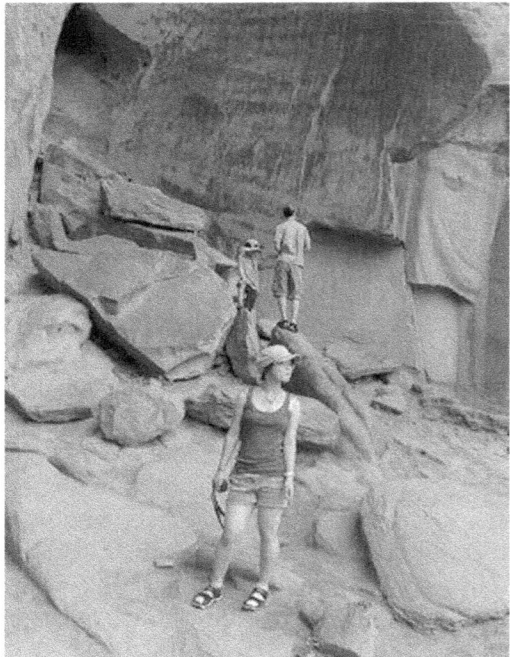

time, and they will see..and together create a beautiful bond called friendship...

My first friendship began with a girl named Julie An. We took the same school bus. I don't clearly remember how we exchanged our first conversations, but I remember exchanging letters with her. Since we both loved to draw, we would always draw something for each other. I met her in my second year of repeating 3rd grade. After finally realizing that my English was undeniably horrible, they had me repeat a year. However, this was a huge turning point in my life.

My teacher was Ms. Charach, and the class was fairly small. I can remember each and every one of my classmate's names and faces. Like last year, Ms. Charach placed me with two translators to help me with my studies, Jason and Mingyuu. Not wanting to repeat the same scary experience as last year, I decided not to bother them with helping me translate everything as much as last year. However, unlike last year, Ms. Charach actually gave me work to do and gave me a vocabulary quiz. Obviously, I got a zero on my first vocabulary test, which was an embarrassing experience. This feeling was worse than getting taunted. No, I felt that my embarrassing grades would soon be the new roots of my taunts. After that test, I studied like a nerd. My mom supported me. I would cheat sometimes by hiding the words under the table while she tested me, and I would get scolded. When the test day finally came, I mounted all of my effort and used it on the test.

When the results finally came in, I was nervous. Ms. Charach would slowly call out each of the student's name, one by one. When she finally called out my name, I slowly reached out for my paper and quickly flipped it over to the back side because I didn't want to see the score. She said something like

"Good job, I'm so proud of you Rei!" but I couldn't understand what it meant at that time. When I slowly, flipped it over, my heart skipped. I saw a one with two zeroes following it. I had earned my first 100%! I was so happy, that I was speechless. When the other students around me saw my grade, they couldn't believe it because those who knew English received lower grades than me. Mingyuu asked me, "Did you cheat?" in Korean. I was dumbfounded and answered back, "What?! NO, I DIDN'T!" He still wouldn't believe me and answered, "C'mon. I won't tell the teacher. You cheated right?" I kept on denying him, and he just gave up in the end, but I still doubt that he believed me. However, I didn't care because I was telling the truth. That time, a girl who sat on the same table congratulated me. Her name was Wen Huang, and we became best friends afterwards. Then, other people began to enter my life.

Trace

While walking down my path, I leave footprints of my presence. It is the proof that I was there and I have retrieved the thing that I have sought in where I once stood. Now it's history and it lives within me…

Upon entering sophomore year of high school, I became

more involved in many school activities. I joined many clubs, teams, and after some thought, joined the JROTC.

JROTC (Junior Reserve Training Corps) is a program for young high school students to strengthen their leadership skills. It was also for people who planned on joining the military as their future career. At first, I was reluctant to join because my friends who were in JROTC were always complaining about how there were inspections every week and how they had to memorize a lot of basic knowledge. Inspection was a weekly routine where we had to wear our uniform and answer some questions that were asked by the inspectors who inspected us.

On my first day of this program, I felt nervous, because I was lost. People were saluting here and there, and the person who stood in the middle, who I guessed was the leader was mumbling something weird to the other person. At first, I didn't think that it was English, but later found out that it was. I already hated it on the first day because they were currently working on a group projects when I joined, and I was also required to do it. The topic of this project was on leadership principles. I had question marks popping out of my head here and there. Group projects never worked out for me because my "partners" never did their part of the assignment. Therefore, I decided to do the PowerPoint myself and told the other guy to work on the skit. Presenting the PowerPoint in front of my class was the hardest part for me. I always became nervous whenever a group of eyes stared at me, all at once. However, this one time, I decided to gather up my courage and thought of it as a first step of changing myself for the better.

When I was done presenting, my AI (army instructor) Sergeant Batts, extolled me for my loud clear voice and my beautiful presentation. I felt a sudden relief of accomplishment at that moment. Throughout the semester, I truly believed that I fit in. My platoon came to respect me and I felt acknowledged and accepted. The next year, I planned to join armed drill which was a team that handled rifles; however, ironically, I ended up joining the Academic team, despite my weakness in academics. Then, irony struck again, when, although this was only my first year on the team, the team commander chose me to compete in the Academic Bowl with four other old team members. I won first place and felt proud. After the competition, people began to misunderstand and thought that I was super smart. I kept on denying it, but knowing that it was a futile effort, I gave up.

After joining JROTC, I also joined the fencing team. The exercises were enduring and painful, but it felt good after practice, despite the sore muscles. I only did drills during my

sophomore year, but in junior year, I finally began to fence. I had great difficulty when it came to form. My fencing stance was weird and the handle was hard to grasp properly. I can clearly blame my previous sport, Tae Kwon Do for my current struggles.

I used to attend the Ultimate Champions Tae Kwon Do Academy back when I was in middle school. I attained black belt and the certificate for it. I also participated in a Tae Kwon Do competition in Queens College where I won a gold medal for both breaking and sparring. Since the Tae Kwon Do forms and techniques were different from that of fencing, I never got better at it. However, I had my own style of fencing.

I was known as the "wild animal" in my fencing team because I bruised everyone in the fencing team and snapped three foils (fencing swords) in half in the process (by accident of course). Whenever I fenced, I just went all out, despite my appalling form. All I cared about was stabbing my opponents for points, and nothing else mattered; whether I won or lost.

I always had a strong sense of denial against losing to a girl. I couldn't accept the fact that another girl was stronger than me. However, through several fights, I swallowed my small pride and came to accept the fact that I was feckless. I had to train myself to become stronger.

My Treasure Chest

What do you seek? Gold and Diamonds to decorate thy pride? Or fame and glory to wave worldwide? Choose either one, but know this...you are a fool to seek such a thing when you already have what is worth a thousand kings. Look deep and you will discover... a treasure chest, yet to be uncovered. Invisible to the naked eyes, but endlessly floating pictures from within...memories...

Throughout my life, I have traveled to many parts of the world. I am an adventurer. My home is each and every land that I explore and make part of me. I met many people whom I knew I would meet again as long as we continue to live under the same sky. Although my memories are blurry, each place has its own significance and still holds a special place in my heart.

Japan, Fukuoka 1994:

Although I was born in Korea, I spent most of my childhood in Japan. I attended school there where every day was nothing but relaxation and fun. In the morning, we would dance and sing to our teacher's piano. In the afternoon, we would eat lunch, play in the playground, then nap. I remember playing with mud, molding it and pretending that it was food and giving it to the teacher to eat (not literally). After waking up from our nap, our parents would come and pick us up. Back then, school was like heaven to me; a place to eat, sleep, and play. Once in a while, the school would hold different festivals. One is the sports festival where they made us run the whole track. I was so close to getting first place, but I regrettably let my guard down in the end. In the same event, I cheer-led and played a game, in which we had to split a watermelon in half with a stick while blindfolded (which I successfully broke). We also had a festival where we wore yukatas and kimonos in the summer. Our class also went on a lot of school trips. One significant one that we went to was to see the sumo wrestlers. The teachers gave us a chance to meet live sumo wrestlers who shook hands with us and swung us with their strong sturdy arms. It

was an interesting experience.

In July 25, 1994, my brother, Brian Park was born. He has the most names in our family. Brian's Japanese name is Yu (which means "to wander off" in Japanese) and he also has two Korean names, Je Song and Sang Shin. He is also called with different names among with his friends; Jason, Brian, Gee, etc... His first ever name was Yu; however, since people made fun of his name by calling out to him, "Hey, Yu! I'm talking to you!" he changed his name and is currently called by the name Brian.

He and I share an interesting relationship. I hate him, and he doesn't care and that is how it works between us. I would beat him and he would go as far as to throwing my wallet out of the window. He feared me, but now that he is bigger and stronger than me, he would take advantage of my short height and fight back. He is a hopeless little fellow and is very immature. It wasn't always like this. We used to be the closest of siblings. We used to hold hands and walk on the flower fields (literally). However, the foreshadowing of this twisted relationship might have been the fact that I hit his face out of curiosity on the first day he was released from the hospital. He was awfully small and red. Truthfully, he looked like an alien, though he turned normal after a while. There are a lot of

127

disagreements between us, but we still get along in the end. There was never logic to our relationship as siblings.

Europe, Denmark 1996:

My days in Japan quickly passed and we followed my dad, who worked as a church minister in Denmark. From there, we traveled to many parts of Europe such as Paris, Sweden, Germany, Norway, Italy, and Switzerland. We also visited many historical places and saw many historical figures. Then, we traveled back to Denmark and settled there, living in the basement of our church. I began to attend the Philips School where I felt like I touched the world for the first time. Although we moved around a lot since I was young, I had always felt like a shadow. I had just followed my parents and never gotten a chance to interact with the people around me with my own voice and mind. This was the beginning of my adventures.

Philips School had no Asians; therefore, I felt awkward and maybe a little different, but the people there accepted me with open arms. I adapted faster than I had thought I would. I learned Danish at an astonishing speed and became friends with several girls my age, and then the whole class. Although I was quiet around the teachers, I became quite popular among the students, especially the girls. The boys in my class used to bully the girls and make them cry, every now and then. However, I would step up every time and chase the boys away and make funny faces to make my friends smile, making the boys laugh at my face as well. We would then play together by building a house with pillows, blankets and cushions. I was also known as the "psychic girl" because I won every luck-and-chance game there was. When our teacher hid a bag of candy somewhere in our classroom, I was the first one to find it and we all got a piece of candy. Back then, we had a popular game of hiding one chalk in either of our hands and guessing which hand the chalk was in. I was the master of this game. I would always guess the right hand, and I became the face of the game. I was proud of my skills, but I didn't think too highly of it at that time.

In front of the school there was a small beach where we went jelly fishing during our snack breaks. The friends whom I usually hung out with Eva, Juana, and Catherina would often challenge one another about who could catch the most jelly fish. I would always win, and we would end up poking the jellyfishes that we had caught together and free them back in the ocean in the end. Back in school, we also had unique school traditions, such as the whole class going to one of the student's house. It was a small class, so it was possible. When Christmas was near, we played Secret Santa and walked around the whole school several times in an angel outfit with each of us holding a candle. During lunch hours, different students were chosen each day to help the teachers make lunch for the students while the other students were watching T.V. When they chose me as their assistant, we sliced apples and carrots into bits of pieces then mixed them together. It was sweet and juicy. We also did peculiar activities during gym periods. Gym was like a trial class. There were no games such as basketball, volleyball, softball, etc… Instead, we had to pass through obstacles that the teacher prepared for us by rolling, jumping, and crawling. In the end, we would be required to climb a rope to ring the bell on top of the ceiling. Sadly and regretfully, I was never able to ring the bell. Despite the fact that I lacked the upper body muscle to drag my heavy body up there, I loved school, along with my friends whom I still keep in touch with, even to this today. When Eva Hansen, one of my best friend from Denmark, sent me a picture of herself, along with her current class picture, I was surprised at how everyone looked so mature, especially Eva. I still feel like a kid compared to them.

In 1997, my sister, Nozomi (meaning "hope" in Japanese), also called Soh-Jong, was born. She was quite big for a baby, but today she is small and skinny. Her nickname is the "Chihuahua" because her eyes are big and round as theirs. Although she is reaching the rebellious age now, she is very obedient and gentle…most of the time. She can get vicious at other times, which is partially my fault. She became influenced by my unladylike nature.

South America, Brazil 1999:

One day, we traveled to Brazil due to a church service that was taking place there. My forty days experience in Brazil was wild. Brazil was a rainy country and there was a forest in front of the place where we lived. Sometimes, poisonous snakes and frogs would come in search of food through the tall grasses, but the men took care of them. I became friends with a girl named Kurenai, whom I met again 10 years later in New York. We lived in the same building and always played together. My most memorable time in Brazil was when we went swimming in a lake full of fishes swimming alongside us. At first, I was scared, but after going inside the water few times, I became used to the fishes pecking my belly and began to chase after the fishes which tried to escape from my grasp. I felt like a fish myself and wished to swim all day long.

After returning to Denmark, my second brother, Ken or Jie-Hyung Park was born. He grew up to be a very sensitive and an irascible little guy. My relationship with my three siblings is very American. They don't address me as unni (the "older sister" title which the younger female siblings use when addressing the older sister) or nuna (the "older sister" title which the younger

male siblings use when addressing the older sister). Therefore, I set up a new rule for them. If they disrespect me, I used to knock some sense into them. I also hate crybabies, so if they cried, I would hit them to make them stop crying. I never thought of this as child or sibling abuse because this was just a way that I showed my "sisterly love" towards them. I believe that this will help them build a stronger character against reality and the people that they would meet in the future. We are very strange, but normal siblings. No matter how many times we fight, I know inside that we still love each other very much.

Japan, Fukuoka 2004:

One summer, I traveled to Japan on my own with my brother, Brian. It was the first time traveling without our parents so, we were both nervous and scared. I followed our plane guide as closely and carefully as possible so that we wouldn't get lost. Although I love to get lost now, back then, I feared being in unfamiliar places. I told my brother to hold on to my back bag strap because he was the type who would wander off easily. One time, while we were still in Denmark, he got lost in the toy store. Fortunately, we found him crying with a group of big men singing together, which I found it to be a very hilarious scene.

I was around twelve when we arrived at Fukuoka Airport. There, we had our little reunion with my grandma, Itoe Fujino and my Uncle, Yousuke Fujino. Children in Japan usually call their grandparents "Obaachyan;" however, since I couldn't pronounce it when I was little, I just called her "Cha." In the end, everyone in the family ended up calling her Cha as well. We also had a unique name for our uncle. Since he has a beard, we call him "Hige no Ojichyan" which is translated into "Uncle with Beard." Of course, they didn't mind, and it was natural for us. I really idolized him because he was smart, rich, and above that, very funny. I remember him tripping Brian and me, while we were running around the house screaming. We fell on the floor laughing while Cha was scolding him. Although he isn't a very sociable type of person, he is very kind and considerate. I have always wished to grow up to be just like him.

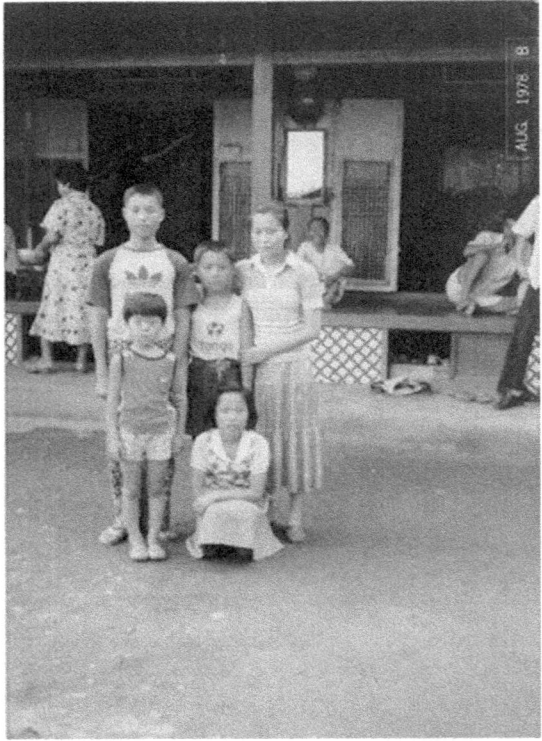

At first, the reunion was a little awkward because we were both very nervous. Not having seen their face for a long time made us feel out of place. At the same time, I felt nauseous and dizzy at first because of the time difference. However, while following the exciting schedule that they had planned out for us, the awkward tension among us vanished, along with my faint feeling.

Our first destination was Moo Moo Land, which was a large farm land consisting of many farm animals and organic daily products. There, I rode a horse that I loved so much and spent the rest of the day spying for cows and other farm animals. Next, we went to the hot springs to refresh ourselves in hot baths. Despite the hot summer in Japan, the bath felt cool for a strange reason. After changing into the yukatas that were prepared for us, we ate a feast of sushi. I felt like a king. Afterwards, my brother and my uncle went to the river to catch fishes. I couldn't tag along because the time difference was coming back to me, making me feel dizzy again. However, I was later entertained by a live, crying cicada that my brother caught on his way back to our room.

The next day, we drove to a big aquarium called Marine World. We explored inside to find many unique and common sea creatures swimming behind their huge glass windows. The most amazing part of this trip was the Dolphin Show. Three dolphin trainers each rode on his or her dolphin's back and swam with them. The dolphins also jumped through big hoops and performed many tricks in the air for each fish that was thrown to them by their trainers. On the same day, we stayed at a hotel near Marine World and gazed into the beautiful sky that night. We watched the fireworks shoot into the sky and bloom into big, beautiful flowers. We had the best view because we witnessed the amazing sky from the beach shore.

After this trip, my uncle had to part ways with us because he had to return to his company. We were a little sad, but I felt that we would see him again soon enough. Throughout the rest of our stay in Japan, Cha took us to various malls in Fukuoka to buy us souvenirs and gifts. She also treated us to my favorite food, putchin pudding, which was like flan, but a little softer than the Spanish ones. We also ate sushi at *Kaiten Sushi*, which was a fun and interesting way to eat sushi. The chef would place the plate with two sushi on the rotating machine. Then, the machine would move in a circular motion, giving us several different plates of sushi to choose from, which we would pick up and eat. The price of our meal depended on which plate we picked up. Each plate had its significant price, and the better the plate was, the better the sushi was.

Afterwards, she took us to her old friend's house. Cha's friends seemed familiar with us, but I didn't remember her very well. Her friends were old couples. The husband couldn't speak very well due to his aging, so I couldn't really understand what he was saying; however, I was touched by his kind expression. When we left their house, I waved to the grandpa as hard and long as I could. I didn't know why but I felt like I had to do this or I would regret it somewhere in my heart. A few years later, I found out through a phone call that he passed away.

Back at home, we joined Cha in a tradition, called the "Obon," where we had to first welcome our ancestors who came down to visit us on earth, then send them back to the sky on smoke. We lit a small fire cracker and as smoke rose from it, we waved our invisible, but present, ancestors goodbye.

America, Florida 2007:

While spending my life in New York, we drove and flew to many parts of America. We went to Washington D.C in 2005 to visit the memorial monument, the White House, and the Lincoln monument. Then, we went to Buffalo to see the Niagara Fall. Few years later, we went to Las Vegas to visit Grand Canyon, Sedona, Monument Valley, Braise Canyon, Zion Canyon, and Death Valley, where the birds were dying and breathing hard with their beaks open from the heat and where there were casinos and gambling everywhere. It was around 102 degrees, there. However, the most impressionable site that I have visited that is still left lingering in my heart with excitement is Disney World.

Upon our arrival in Florida, I felt a wave of warm air gently breezing across my face. Florida was a very hot and a tropical state. The sky was clear blue with palm trees scattering the illuminating light. I loved the house that we rented to stay in. Inside were our own private swimming pool, a game of Pool, a table tennis and large rooms with multiple TVs and large beds to relax on. To make things better, there was cool air conditioning inside. After unpacking our luggage, we left for Disney World.

Disney World was separated into four main theme parks; Magic Kingdom, Animal Kingdom, Hollywood Studios, and Epcot. During our ten days stay, we explored a different station, each day. First, we visited Epcot, which has a big golf ball like icon called the Spaceship Earth beyond the entrance. Epcot is divided into Future World and World Showcase. Future World focuses on technological advancements and innovations while World Showcase is a Pavilion containing shops, attractions and restaurants that represent the culture and cuisine of eleven countries; Mexico, Norway, China, Japan, France, Italy, Germany, United States, Canada, Morocco, and United Kingdom. Since, it was July 4th on one of the days of our stay, we were able to see a show called, "The Illumination Reflection," near the lake that was in the center of Epcot. The show consisted of fireworks with springs and flames bursting from the lake. There were also music and moving mascots. It was the most amazing fireworks that I have witnessed in my whole life. It was a magical night.

Our next trip was to Animal Kingdom. It was like a real jungle. There were palm trees and ivies everywhere. We also saw animals behind their cages sun bathing, while the others were exhausted from the heat. The rides were breathtaking. One ride had a Jurassic Park theme, and we rode a truck while Dinosaurs screeched and leered at us. Before this ride, I never knew a ride so real existed in this world. While walking and deciding on our next ride, I saw a small movement among one of the trees. I thought it was my imagination, until I saw a face, painted green, hiding among the forest green vines. Then, she released the tree that she was hugging and began to walk towards us. To my surprise, there were more of them, one by one unraveling themselves and walking into our view. They were walking on a tall stick-like objects which were hidden by vines. I wondered how they were able to stand and balance themselves on such a thin stick.

Our next destination was Hollywood Studios. It had an environment of that of a movie set. There were live shows of blockbuster movies with epic stunts like Indiana Jones; thrilling attractions, such as The Hollywood Tower Hotel, which was a haunted hotel with hunted elevators and spirits of the dead, and the Rock'n Roller Coaster which was the fastest roller coaster that I rode in my life. We also took photos with the Disney characters such as Mickey Mouse and Goofy. Other entertainments included the illuminating night show *Fantasmic* and the Character Greetings around the theme park. I saw Jack Sparrow from the Pirates of Caribbean whom I really wanted to take pictures with, but in the end, gave up because there was an impossibly large crowd surrounding him. Luckily, I was able to take a picture with my old favorite character, the Winnie the Pooh.

Finally, we visited the Magic Kingdom where dreams and magic came true while fairy tales came to life. At night, we saw the *"Spectro Magic"* Parade where Mickey and his friends, along with the Disney Princesses waved to us on their carriages. Although by glimpse, I saw Tinkerbell fly out from Cinderella's Castle. Disney World felt like a place where my world became reality. I doubted that a place like this existed, but I was wrong, and it opened my eyes to the possibilities of this world.

Korea, Seoul/ Japan, Tokyo 2008:

On an account in hearing the depressing news of my grandma's death, we went to Korea and Japan. The purpose of this trip was to visit all of my family members before any misfortune befalls them. When my grandma from my Dad's side passed away, I didn't know what to feel. We didn't see each other for ten years; therefore, I didn't feel the big loss. However, a part of me was sad and wished to see her at least one more time. We first went to Korea, Seoul, my hometown, to visit our grandma's grave.

After that, we visited our aunts, uncles, cousins, and great grandmas. Like Japan, Korea was a little awkward to me at first because ten years passed from the last time I visited Korea. I wasn't familiar with any of my aunts, uncles, and my cousins. The fact that I didn't really get along with Koreans made this reunion more complicated. However, when we arrived, they treated us with great care and hospitality. They prepared us with

many delicious foods and gifts for us to take back to New York. Since my Dad's older brother lent us his car, we were able to drive to Pusan, Kyongju, Pohang, Yongdok, Wonju, Seoul, Kapyong, Chongju, Kwangju, Posong, Yosu, Hwaomea, Hampyong, Chyongpyong and Korean Folk Village.

We also went to my dad's birthplace, Kwang Yang which now looked ancient and old. There were tall grasses growing everywhere and the house was covered in spider webs. Now, dusts and small creatures lived inside the house, but it was still there, which I think is amazing. A front of the house was a small ocean. Luckily, it was a tide when we got there and we saw small fishes jumping up and down with their tails and crabs bubbling and hiding underneath the shells. The water was slowly beginning to return, but in the meantime, I enjoyed standing on the damp dirt and sand where the ocean water once covered. After our short but long trip, I began to feel more comfortable in Korea. At the same time, I learned and memorized the faces of my aunts, uncles, and cousins. I was surprised to find myself with so many cousins, at first, I didn't know who was related to whom or whose daughters and sons they were. We didn't know what to say to them because they only spoke Korean, and they seemed speechless around us as well. Nevertheless, in the end, we all got along; especially by younger brother and Grace's little brother, Samming Park. Grace Park is one of my cousins who is currently living in New York with us. She came all the way from Seoul to study English. Unlike me, she caught on fast to her new environment. Her bright and sociable character also helped her get along with her new classmates and my family. I sometimes envied her determination and studiousness.

Next we visited our grandma who lived alone in Japan, Cha. After we visited several friends there, we went to Tokyo to meet my mom's brother who worked in the Asahi Glass Company that researched several types of special glasses. Since this was my first time in Tokyo, I enjoyed my first tour around it. We visited the Rainbow Bridge, the Tokyo Tower, and old shrines. Although not as big from here, we saw the famous Mount Fuji from the top of the Tokyo Tower. In the end, our uncle took us to a big hot spring building in Yokohama. There, we changed into yukatas and after a long refreshing break in the sauna and the hot spring, we explored the different floors to find a game center, a restaurant, and a huge TV room with comfortable chairs to sleep on. The next morning, we woke up very early to take a last hot dip in the bath and to see the huge Ferris wheel that was outside the building that we stayed in. In the end, we watched the morning sun rise as our trip came to an end.

Korea, Seoul/ KAYAC 2009:

During the summer, after my trip to Las Vegas, I was accepted into the Korean American Program, called KAYAC. It is a program for Koreans, who do know or understand much about their own heritage, either because they were born in America or because they had spent most of their life in America. We were to hand in an essay based on why we wanted to go to Korea. Only a few people's essays were accepted. The people who passed the first round moved onto the second round, which consisted of a short test and an interview. I had doubted that I would get in; however, surprisingly, they accepted me, and I was in group one. During the month of July, I and the other 69 people

who were accepted flew to Korea to learn about our culture, tradition, and history. It was the best experience that I've ever been through. We stayed at one of the top Korean universities, the Koryo University (otherwise known as Korea University), and visited a lot of famous places, such as KBS, military campus, and museums.

When we arrived, tour buses were waiting for us outside of the airport. We moved as a group and with our suitcases, boarded the bus. The insides of the buses were not like the insides of any other buses that I rode before. There were purple curtains with beads on top of the windows and rainbow lights on top of the bus ceiling. There was also a karaoke system with a huge TV screen in the front, including a micro phone. In the bus, I became friends with a girl named Mira Kim, who was in the same group as me. She became my bus buddy, but my roommate was a different girl from a different group. Her name was Stacy Gil. Coincidently, I met her before in a SAT school named KENT. She remembered me as well, and I found her to be very friendly and outgoing.

At first, I was nervous, but in the end, I was glad that she was my roommate. The dorm itself was great as well. Inside each room were two beds, a bathroom and a connected study table. We even had refrigerator in our room. It was fairly neat and nice. There were about twelve floors in all. The basement was sort of like a relaxing room. There were computers, a TV screen, a comfortable couch to sit on, and a small deli for some midnight snack, such as cookies and ice cream. Unfortunately, I was too cheap to buy anything. As for meal, we had to walk to another building to eat breakfast, lunch, and dinner on the days we stayed in the campus. Each meal was a buffet, and it was surprisingly delicious. A part of my daily routine during my trip was morning exercises. Every morning, I woke up at six and met up with the teachers who led one of the seven groups.

One morning, during our stay in a hotel, I woke up and since nobody else was awake, I went to the exercise room alone. Then, my group teacher, Sun Jeoung Kwon, came in. We both decided to sneak out and to take a walk outside of the hotel since everybody else was still asleep and there were still time left before breakfast. We walked around Jong Ghe Jong where the stones that we walked on were vey shiny and organized. During our walk, she explained to me about the place, and then, she began to ask me about my family. It was a little awkward at first because whenever she asked me something, I had to form a complete answer in my head before I replied back to her. Overall,

it turned out to be a very interesting walk together. We decided to keep our little walk a secret from the other students because they weren't able to explore the bridge due to the lack of time and the rainy weather.

It was a great experience. Unfortunately, it lasted for only ten days and afterwards, I went to stay with my family in Korea, who welcomed me warmly, for another ten days.

I had departed to Korea in search of my identity. Before finding the existence of this program, I had hesitated on whether I could proudly state that I am Korean without a doubt in my mind. I knew too little about the Korean culture, environment, food, language, etc. to have confidence in my nationality. What does it really mean to be a Korean? Could I make Korea a place where I could always turn to?

Upon my return from Korea, I was able to see Korea for what it truly was. Before this trip, the word "Korea" seemed plain like a painting without colors. I only thought about the fact that my family lives there and that it was my birth place. However, after this journey, my image of Korea expanded.

Truthfully, I didn't know how to make Korean foods such as kimbab and bibimbab before this trip. I also never realized that Korea was developing several high technologies, such as moving photos, touch commands, and instant food machines. KBS was also an interesting place. For the first time in my life, I was able to see real movie stages and celebrities. The military camp left another breathtaking impression on me. We saw tanks and several types of guns and gears. For the first time, I got a chance to go inside the tank, which was a little crowded and learned how to control it. Next, they took us to a tunnel in which they used to shoot their targets and move around with less risk of getting killed. Then, we approached a tower where they kept their eyes out for their enemies. It took great effort to climb up the long hill and climb back down on our feet, but it was worth the experience. We were able to see the fence that separated North Korea and South Korea on our way down. Although it may not have been a memorable experience for everyone, I think that it was amazing. Back at the campus, we drew Korean flags and learned what each symbol symbolized and also played a Quiz game on our second to the last day.

During this trip, I was given several chances to have conversations in Korean. First, I exchanged a few words in Korean with friends who were in the same confused state as I was. Then, after a few days, I began to talk to the teachers as if they were my friends. It was a little more challenging when it came to my relatives; however, I believe that they understood my messages to them. Surprisingly, to prove that my effort was worth it, when I returned from Korea, an individual from my church told me that my Korean improved. I felt very accomplished when I heard that.

As a result of this trip, I began to listen to more Korean pop music such as "Fire" and "Heartbeat" that I had not even thought about listening to before. I also began to watch Korean dramas like 선덕여왕 because of the Korean commercial previews that I was drawn to. I even began searching for some Korean foods that I ate during my stay in Korea that I had never eaten here before.

A certain lady asked me during this trip whether I felt if it was ever possible for there to be peace between Korea and Japan. That was when I knew that another source of my hesitation came from my other half of my identity, which was also a part of me. I didn't know the answer then, and I still don't;

now, however, my instincts tell me that it is possible if future leaders lend their hands to one another to create a new bond. The past cannot be changed, but the future can with effort, and if possible, I would like to play a role in it.

I still lack in several parts of my identity; therefore, instead of limiting myself to only this experience, I would like to participate in other activities that can help complete my incomplete self.

Now, I don't have to doubt my identity, but just build it up with more experience and knowledge. I've learned that Korea is a country of high pride and spirit of nationalism and I am proud to be from such a wonderful nation.

I Quit, I'm Going to Become a Pirate

The darkness that roams around our hearts, we accept so openly with no control or thought. It feeds on our scars and is bred within the seven sins... pride... wrath... envy... greed... gluttony... sloth... lust... We gave birth to them, letting them eat our heart away is an easy task...but why does it feel so sad? We still try to reach out for the shattered lights, piercing through our hearts and trickling tears that longs for warmth and laughter. Here we lie waiting in the darkness, for someone to find us and break these burdened chains. Unlocking the doors within and spreading our wings, under the vast blue sky, we smile...when there's darkness there is also light...

Have you ever wished to become or go somewhere you know you can never possibly go to? Have you ever thought about wanting to become a pirate, hunting for treasure chests or maybe even flying across Never Land where you are free from rules and time? Growing up was a never friendly idea to me. School became harder, my parents became stricter, and I was banned from having any fun. My life seemed to become darker and duller as time passed. My spirit didn't agree with my maturing body and the hard reality; the world was made up of numbers and academics.

This all began when I entered high school. Like in every school that I attended, I was academically slow, the first year. I wasn't failing, but I was what people called, "Asian failing." Sophomore year I became one of the smart students with report cards of A+s, whom people came to respect. Then, the deadly junior year came. My grades went downhill and uphill, and finally downhill. My worst subject was math. Although I was passing geometry with flying colors, I failed trigonometry with equally flying colors. Due to the huge difference in my grades from my sophomore year to junior year, whenever I failed a test, my friends looked at me as if I wasn't feeling well or as if something was wrong with me. I didn't mind, though it got annoying once in a while. But what hurt more than their reactions was my depressingly low grades. I never knew until I entered high school that numbers could hurt me. Low grades meant cold eyes from the teachers and limited freedom.

I was the type of girl who wouldn't even spend a dollar on a snack or anything. Whenever I received money, I would save it up in my little envelope safe and hide it from my siblings who tend to steal my money. No matter how much I wanted something, I learned to hold back my feeling of desire of necessities. However, I couldn't stop my parents from spending thousands of dollars on my studies, academics, and my necessities. Despite my powerlessness I would complain and tell them to stop wasting so much money. They would answer, "Who do you think we're spending money for!?" "Instead of worrying about our money, start studying so that it wouldn't go to the waste!" I hated to admit it but they were right. If I was more responsible, then they wouldn't have to spend so much extra money on me. Yet, I asked for more, leading me to a feeling of sharp guilt.

I hated myself for being selfish, and I was angry with myself for being so ignorant of my parent's burdens and stress. I would cry in silence in the basement, not because I was scolded for my lack of progress, but because my parents would blame themselves for my and my sibling's mistakes and actions. I was frustrated with myself. If I called myself stupid, they would take

it as calling our family ancestors stupid. They can't understand my thoughts, but I didn't blame because I knew myself that my character was a little complicated. My need for them to understand me was just one of my selfish desires. As I ran outside to let out all my stress, I complained to myself that this world labeled everything depending on an individual's grade and potential and abandoned anyone who didn't meet its expectations. In front of our house, there is a big tree that could suck out my explosive emotions. I kicked it, punched it, and banged my head against it until I calmed down. After getting lectured, I would go to sleep because I lose my ability to concentrate. Then, my mom

145

would tell me to stop running away from reality. Everything was different, and I didn't know how to go back.

When I think that what I do now affects my future, I become afraid and lose my mind, even though I know that that won't get me anywhere. I can imagine my future, but can't see it, like blurry colors mixed together without a concrete picture of what I want to see. My basic idea of my future is to marry someone arranged by my parents (which I don't mind) and to have children. The rest of my imagination comprises of living in a big house with decent income and days filled with fun. I found myself become very pessimistic over the years.

After several thoughts, I realized something. While in my mother's womb, I was surrounded by darkness until light found me. If this is true, then I will see that light again. The sun may be covered by the dark clouds, but nothing can cover the dark clouds. If it is hidden, we just need to find it. Happy times may end and it may be impossible to go back in time, but sad times are the same and will also eventually come to an end.

I have many dreams that I hope to accomplish in the future and one of those dreams is to travel around the world and meet new people. I love to experience things that are beyond reality such as magic and mystical creatures. I won't hide the fact that I love day dreaming. I often think of myself on a pirate ship setting on sail in search of treasures. I may sound childish, but I really believe that this is possible and can say proudly that this is the best trait that I have of myself; creating my own world.

Thank You

People seek satisfaction, their own happiness, blinding themselves from the people around them. What is happiness? Is it to bring warm bright smiles to others while sacrificing your own chance of happiness? Or is it to fill your unfulfilled desires and care about your own penance? This brings about another question. What are desires? Here I stand, looking down while asking these endless questions. If I ask one question, another one follows. Instead, why not look forward and start taking steps towards the future? Time won't wait for us, but we can turn time

into our ally. There are many closed paths before us, and we are standing on the center of them all. Within us, we have the keys to open these doors. We may not have it in our hands yet, but we can create them.

On the way, we may stumble upon boulders and may be forced to take the longer way to our goal. We may even drop something and never see it again or break into thousands of pieces by the force of our emotions. Yet, the pieces will always come together in the end to form new hope. Like a puzzle piece, if you find that a piece is missing from the picture, why not create a piece to complete it instead of giving up?

Everyone has desires and wants to be satisfied, but what is wrong with that? We are human, and desire is something that is born from within us and continues to live within us. It is like our baby, but also a beast. We must nurture it and tame it and make it beautiful. It is ok to be selfish and chase after your own happiness. Your roots of guilt and uneasiness will understand, as long as you don't get controlled by the ugly side of your desires.

What makes me shine? I am still searching, through the dark clouds of enigma... Still looking for my door, my light, my dream... like a lost child. One day I will pierce through the dark sky with my arrow and aim for the light. Then, my path will clear and I will be found...I will find what I am looking for...

We are all afraid of rejection, so we don't say this. It is much safer and easier to say "I'm sorry," and end it. Kindness is cruel. We never asked for it, yet we want it. It confuses our feelings towards that person. In the end, not everyone may be lined up smiling...however, let me bring out my courage, just this once and say this, hoping that it will ring in your heart forever...thank you for loving me...

"My Dream"
Daniel Hong

I was born on June 23, 1993, in Saint John's Hospital, located in New York, and was named after Saint Daniel. I also have a Korean name: Sae Hoon. To Koreans, it means "Teacher of the world", but to others it doesn't mean anything. My mom told me that of all of her three sons, I was the one who gave her the most pain during labor. I, like all babies, cried loudly when born, even though a birth is supposed to symbolize rapture and mirth. A year after I was born, I moved into a house in Paramus, New Jersey, where I spent the next decade.

I am "the cream in the Oreo cookie" of my family. I am the middle child of three sons and have to cope with the responsibilities that I have over my little brother, Steven and my older brother, Chris. I consider myself lucky to have two brothers

Growing up, I was attached to the outdoors and the adventures I had with my neighbors and friends. We would play outside in the resplendent sun until we would get tanned to a rich brown in the summer and get bright red cheeks in the winter. We would think that we were the fastest and the strongest people in the world, except for our dads, of course. We would sit at the end of our block for the ice cream truck and shout in glee when it showed up; however, our joy was all in vain because we would beg our mothers for money.

I remember when I learned how to ride a bicycle. I saw all of the other kids riding them and was determined to ride also. But learning to ride a bike came with injuries and constant falls. I, like all bicyclists, learned how to ride a bike the hard way, considering there is no easy way. It looked so easy but it actually required time-worthy skill. And after many failed attempts, I finally achieved liftoff. I was finally doing it; it felt as if I was flying, and it felt exhilarating.

My dream? To some it may seem as if my dream only consists of me being wealthy, but it is much more than that. My dream is a dream that not only benefits me, but finally provides eternal relief to my parents. My father says his dream is to have only one week of vacation from work. Some might consider this a long period of time, but my father never missed a day of work. I have a great respect for my father. I hope to be as assiduous as my father. And I would like to provide him with a comfortable retirement, in which he could go wherever he wants and enjoy the fine things he was not able to enjoy as he worked daily to support me and my brothers and our futures.

I am a shy guy who has grown steadily in confidence and skill. I remember how shy I was as a boy.

I had a cute crush on a Korean girl when I was in the first grade, which lasted until the day I moved to another town. Being very shy and timid as a little fledgling, I would show my liking to her through discreet actions, such as giving her two pieces of chocolate for Valentine's Day when I had given everybody else only one piece.

After third grade, I left all of my friends and neighbors and moved to my current residence Montvale, New Jersey. I attended Memorial Elementary School and I remember for my first day of school, I was very late and went into the building only knowing which room my class was in. I finally found my classroom, stepped in, and saw a room full of students and my new teacher. I quickly made new friends and felt accepted. The only problem was that I was not familiar with Spongebob Squarepants because I did not have cable in my house. Even though this does not seem like a big issue, it was a great issue for everyone. Not knowing Spongebob was like not knowing who George Washington was. But I was able to gain acceptance through other means. I soon earned the title as the fastest kid in my class, after playing football in my gym period with my class; a title I held very proudly.

I was never really good at presentations. During my elementary and middle school years, I would be distraught about having to present a project in front of the whole class. My earliest experience was when my teacher assigned a "fun"

project and handed out the grading rubrics; the page was littered with expectations. We had 3 weeks to build a model of buildings or structures that people used to make, such as pyramids or the Eiffel Tower. We even had to talk for 4 to 5 minutes to the class about our model. I chose to build an igloo. With glue and marshmallows, I applied all of my ten-year-old brainpower to make one and produced a disheveled and clumsily made igloo.

During the day of the presentation, I brought my creation and awaited my name to be announced. I looked around to see that all of the other kids' creations were flawless, immaculate, and so much better than mine. Ms. Gray, my fifth grade teacher, asked if anyone wanted to go first and that if no one wanted to go first she would randomly choose a student. No one volunteered, and when Ms. Gray was randomly choosing, I prayed to God that she would not select me, and God answered my prayer. When others presented, they did not seem nervous at all nor did they falter in their speech. Not soon after, it was finally my turn. I presented with a shaky voice and crimson-red face, and kept wondering when the ordeal was going to finish, but after a long 5 minutes, it was finally over. And this was one of the first memories of my school education.

As I transitioned to the middle school, Fieldstone Middle School, I found a new friend who was in the same class as I, my cousin, Andrew. It felt very strange to have one of my best cousins attending the same classes as me, but it offered me a safeguard, a friend whom I could always talk to and understand.

I was introduced to the clarinet through the band program of Fieldstone, and I am relieved that I was so lucky to have been part of the program. I chose to play it not only because it looks aesthetically appealing, but because my older brother, Chris, also chose to play it. During seventh-grade, I begged my mom to let me take guitar lessons and to buy me a guitar. And after arguing with her for a full week, I ended up victorious, and to this day I do not regret learning the guitar.

Playing the guitar is fun, but learning *how* to play it and overcome the obstacle of taming it is even more fun. Learning how to play an instrument is like taming a wild animal, once tamed one can do tricks with it and have it mastered. Currently, I lead praises at St. Joseph's Roman Catholic church, during the main mass time on Sundays, utilizing my guitar skills. St. Joseph's Roman Catholic Church is a Korean Catholic church in Demarest, Bergen County, New Jersey, and one of the biggest Korean Catholic churches in the United States.

Being a Korean-American made it hard for me to identify myself as either Korean or American, and even harder to say which identity I liked more. My 13th summer was also the first time I had been on a plane, so I asked my friends what it was like. Some said it was fun, while others, scary. But for me, it seemed like a rollercoaster; a 14 hour ride that started at Newton, New Jersey, but unlike a rollercoaster, one does not end at one\s initial position but rather in a land thousands of miles from home. I was far more interested in the plane ride than Korea, and felt that Korea was just as much to me as a relative whom I've never seen before in my life.

Arriving in the foreign land, I felt fatigued from what I came to know as "jetlag". Upon arriving, I immediately tried to call my friends with long-distance calling but was disappointed to learn that Korea's time was 13 hours ahead of America's time and that they were most probably sleeping. I felt misplaced and not the norm, like I was on the wrong side of the map. When my "cousin", a teenager whom I have never seen in my life, offered me noodles, I asked for a pizza, and when I greeted my aunts and uncles, I would wave to them instead of bowing respectfully. Soon after getting settled, my mother had me attend the school there, so I could learn the culture and get to know the students.

The schools were drastically different from the schools in America. You had to wear sandals in the building, and there were no janitors, so the students were the ones who had to clean the school. There was also library time, a time when we all go to the library and read famous literature. I was very illiterate in Korean so I was the "special student" who read the children books in Korean and only read the "hard" English books. I also spoke the language with a very heavy American accent and with horrible Korean, so bad that it was almost impossible to understand what I was saying. So, to communicate I used an American-Korean Translator.

During recess, I was surprised that not one person in the entire school was familiar with football. I'm not talking about the soccer football, but the American football. After explaining the game, I was surprised by their responses. They thought tackling and attacking the opponent, like a military operation, were far too dangerous to be called a sport. Despite all of this, the students respected me because I was from America, and anticipated that America had only good things to offer. In the end, to them I was representing America, and all I wanted to do was go back home to the United States. I hated showering two times a day because of the 100-degree climate, talking about America, and eating the same foods every day, and was frustrated at myself for not being able to identify myself better, due to my lack of Korean language skills.

The doldrums all changed when my parents took my brothers and me to the countryside of Korea to stay a few days. Once there, we walked to a hillside with lots of food and stopped at a lump in the ground. My parents were setting up the food and seemed to be praying to this lump. 'What is this?' I asked; it is the grave of my grandfather. He passed away before my mother was born and asked to be buried in the countryside of Seoul, his home. Home. I then realized that home was not just one's country or one's identity but was where one feels most secure and was cognizant that my home was not Korea or America but with my family.

Within the three months, two weeks, and five days I have stayed in Korea, I learned to appreciate my surroundings and my environment. I eventually spoke Korean better and a little more fluently and was so accustomed to the food that I craved kimchi and noodles instead of pizza and French fries.

And as quickly as I came to love my native country, the more rapid did my trip to Korea come to a conclusion. I was so attached to the apartment at which I had stayed that I called it home, but I knew that I had to return to America.

The plane trip to America was the second time I had been on a plane, but I was far more concerned about leaving my country. The plane ride took 14 hours, and I would arrive back at the house. It took me so long to realize that I was neither Korean nor American, but a Korean-American. The plane ride back to America did not seem like a rollercoaster ride, which is turbulent and unsettled, but was like cruising on a highway back from a new place I can call home.

I grew six inches by the end of that summer and I was as tall as my friends. My middle school experience was fleeting and flew by quickly but I was strongly influenced by my band teacher, Dr. Sommers. He was everyone's favorite teacher and this was not just coincidence. He always helped anyone who was in need and treated everyone with a respect and equality that made him a great teacher and this is the only reason why I am playing second chair of my high school concert band.

After 4 quick years of middle school, I finally graduated, a new experience with emotions that were mixed with nostalgia, sadness, and excitement. And high school came right around the corner. It was in some kind of sense a new excitement and experience but I knew my performance in high school could ultimately determine my future. I was very eager to test my ability and knowledge to enroll into a good college.

It was during my high school experience that I joined the Chemistry Olympics team with my friends Jinhoo and Tony where my team and I won the bronze medal after countless hours of hard work and commitment. Our daunting task was to construct a solar water heating device that would produce the largest efficiency. From November to May, my team and I came together every week to brainstorm, build at the engineering room, and even shop for items. In May, we presented our model to judges and competed with at least 15 other teams. When the announcer awarded us our medals, I felt pride, nostalgia, and remorse that such a great learning experience had ended. With my coaches, Mr. Soltmann and Ms. Macke, standing proud, I gladly received the medal and felt very accomplished – not to mention tired.

In high school, I realized that many people were just there to obtain only grades to go to college; however, Pascack Hills was more than just the letter I received on my report card; it was also the people I met along the way that made my high school experience the best life experience I could ever have.

"A Real-Life Movie Masterpiece"
Grace Chun

I like to think of my life as a movie – a series of motion pictures that fit together like a puzzle. There exists a rising action, which consists of the build-up of relationships, character, and experiences. Next, the climax occurs when a sudden and unexpected change occurs. Turmoil. Success. Devastation. Reward. Failure. Whatever the situation, the climax turns the tide of the entire movie and produces new revelations for the character. Then, the music dies down and the falling action takes place. Will the character be defeated? Will she overcome her conflicts? The rest of the movie depends upon the fate of the character and how she chooses to live out her life. My movie does not end in that electrifying true love's kiss, nor does it fit one particular genre. It is action, thriller, drama, and adventure, all rolled up into one.

509 Douglas Drive. This is where it all began – the start of an idyllic childhood. A young girl of about ten years old walks out of her front porch in her quaint, suburban neighborhood. Her hair is streaked with unnatural blonde highlights and her chubby, round face is sprinkled with unique characteristics. Her sandy skin, serene eyes, plump cheeks, and small nose define her. Her hair is combed back to perfect pigtails, which frame both sides of her face. She is wearing her favorite shirt – a bright white tank with glittery tropical letters that say "Angel" across the chest. She is a zealous tomboy at heart. It is a normal day for her as she walks hand in hand with her sister to school, Kingston Elementary, the place where she would one day look back upon with great nostalgia. Fifth grade. Ms. King. The nascent stages of her observant mind. This character was none other than myself, as a young girl stepping out into a new world of wonder and awe. Ms King, my fifth grade teacher, was quite the character. Her hawkish nose, piercing brown eyes, withered hair, thin lips, bony structure, and peculiar voice amazed me. Her brash and merciless demeanor was intriguing to me, though everyone else despised her for it. I was completely drawn to my surroundings; my curious spirit made me want to experience everything, and I anticipated it like the crucial

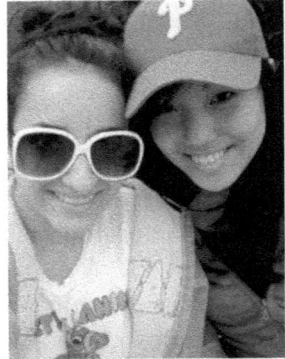

moments before un-wrapping a fresh, untainted piece of candy. Ms. King's voice rings in my head even today. As a young girl, it reminded me of the voice of Ms. Fowl from the cartoon, "The Adventures of Jimmy Neutron", squawking across the classroom relentlessly. Whether it was mastering a stroke of cursive handwriting, or learning about the formation of rocks, I was introduced to a world outside of my own from her class, and I could let my mind wander into unknown territories.

The miniscule details are what I remember the most about fifth grade. The stifled smell of cough drops, bland walls, Ms. King's stubby, illegible handwriting on the chalkboard. I was consumed by the endless days of elementary school. I was diligent in my studies and always worked hard for my goals; this dedication was not for a college scholarship, the approval of my parents, a successful future, or a 4.0 GPA, rather, it was for my own satisfaction in filling my unwrinkled brain with new information. Ms. King's class introduced me to feelings of competition, incompetence, pride, and success, and opened my eyes to people and relationships. I was ambitious, and the title of "Best Cursive Handwriting" was all I ever wanted from life as an eager fifth grader.

My movie shifts to a scene of adventure. Not only was my childhood filled with school, but it was also consumed with family and friends. They are the ones who brought adventure into my life- adventure that created a beatific world, a solid family life, and friendships filled with spontaneity.

The main character walks into a white and brick church that towers above her small body. It is a snowy wonderland and the vast field in front of the church is covered with a deep, soft blanket of snow, and the majestic church building is adorned with winter white hats. The air is grey, rigid, peaceful, and still. The distant sound of children gaily laughing can be heard.

One particular experience in my life that defines my childhood adventure was my time at church. As the daughter of a pastor, I grew up going to church every week, sometimes even two or three times a week. In this particular snowy milieu, I remember stepping out onto that never-ending field in front of my church (it would stretch all the way down to a house that we thought was haunted). It was an eternal playground. Snowy Sundays were the best, because all of my church friends and I would build forts-girls against boys and have snow fights. We created imaginary snowball-making factories and diligently produced countless snowballs while our hands lost circulation. Every week was a new adventure for me. That field symbolized my freedom, carefree days, and the extent of my imagination. In the summer, we would make mud balls, play with sticks to make fire and play tackle football.

In the fall, we would gather up all the leaves, jump in them, get out with bugs clinging onto our church clothes, get out, and do it all over again. Sylvia Lee, Aimee Jung, Esther Kang, Crystal Lee, Christina Lee, Isaac Chong, Danny Jung, Phill Pae, Andrew Pae- just to name a few, these individuals were, and some still are, like my brothers and sisters. At a young age, I did not understand the real purpose of going to church. Nonetheless, my adventurous life began at church, where I could be free and unguarded amongst my friends.

Then and now, my relationships are very similar. However, the natural cycle of life has come into play. Now, it is not a matter of how many times we can jump into a pile of leaves, but who would be watching to criticize our behavior. Reality is like a movie because the outside world is constantly watching your life and how you live it. For myself, this was magnified as the daughter of a pastor, but it made me realize how much I appreciate my family.

Drama. My parents are brave individuals. Some may label them as typical Korean parents who sacrifice their lives for their children, and this is true. But at the same time, their ability to speak words of wisdom, bear pain and suffering, and love unconditionally, even in times of greatest adversity, proves the extent of their sacrifice. Drama is a constantly occurring aspect that my father has to deal with as a pastor, but as the head of the family, he chooses to keep it all to himself and bear the burden. It brings me the greatest sorrow when I see my strong parents fall weak and powerless to the harm inflicted upon them by others. The murmur of their voices in the living room after a long Sunday, their blank expressions, forced words, and look of helplessness indicate when something is wrong at church. Nonetheless, they never give up; their struggles motivate them to push us – my older brother, sister, and myself – to succeed and fulfill everything we set our minds to.

Though some moments of my movie are solemn and the characters face much hardship, moments of success often procede. Thus, my life is a thriller because of the emotional rollercoaster, the unexpected twist of events, and monumental experiences that I encounter. In the setting of my movie, the tense and stifled atmosphere of drama fades, the music becomes suspenseful, whetting the attention of the audience.

The character is seen stepping into a classroom with blinding lights, three nameless judges, and a music stand. She has a warm flute in her hand from the extended warm-up session; the flute slides down her wet, sweaty hands as she makes her way step by step across the tense room. She inhales a deep, forced breath of the musty air that smells of old textbooks. The room is still, and the commencement of life depends solely upon her. A gulp of bland saliva. Trembling hands. She closes her eyes. Her notes sing out gracefully; they are pure and golden, and resonate throughout the frozen world. Hindemith's *Sonate* is the name of the piece, but she plays as though Grace's *Sonate* would be more apt. All the while, her untamed heart is pumping rapidly like a snare; the music in her veins flow throughout her body and into her soul.

This crucial experience describes my audition for the All South Jersey Band on the flute. Ever since the fourth grade, music was a great part of my life. In actuality, music was instilled upon me by my pianist mother as a very young child, but piano was not for me. In truth, I chose the flute because there was nothing else that was fit for me – the saxophone was too big, the clarinet was taken by my sister, and the violin was taken by my brother. The only common instrument left for me was the flute. However, as I got older, I learned to appreciate the art of the flute, even though there were moments when I completely abhorred it. After practicing, my arms would ache and my fingers would become frozen, but some of my greatest moments of success are attributed to these experiences. I made it into the All South Jersey Band throughout middle school and most of high school. Though it may not be a huge accomplishment for some, this achievement symbolized all of my hard work and sacrifices paying off. The truth that one must always work for his or her goals became a reality to me.

As I became acquainted with high school and matured as a tenth grader, the world around me suddenly became so much larger. During the summer, I went on a mission's trip to the Dominican Republic, where the action portion of my movie takes place. Though the typical action genre consists of fast cars, stunts, and gunshots, my action segment involves helping a community in the Dominican Republic. The mission's team consisted of fourteen people, including myself. Isaac Chong, Sunah Park, Duksoo Park, Phill Pae, Esther Kang, Jennifer Chun, Jane Han, Yeana Chung, John Han, Joe Woo, Jae Yu, Dr. Lee, and Pastor Brian Park are the names of the other individuals of the mission team. As members of the Cherry Hill Presbyterian Church, we were already like a family but grew even closer together from the mission's training and service.

We stayed at a church called "La Esperanza", which means "Hope". It was a small, one-roomed church. As one might expect, the people of the community were deprived of many amenities; however, they were not deprived of

their passionate spirit for God. Their upbeat songs of praise and dedication to the church contrasted with the strife-filled crime and poverty in the community. We helped out with the Vacation Bible School (VBS) and led skits, songs, and dances for two hundred or three hundred kids in one packed room.

The air was unbearable and hot, but everyone was shouting from the top of their lungs and singing. I helped distribute clothes, candy, and drinks afterward to the kids. Often, kids from neighboring villages would try to enter the church for the free food and clothes, and it could become dangerous. Nonetheless, the entire experience taught me so much about the world and my mission; I had the opportunity to serve children who lived entirely different lives. The pastor and his wife who were there were so giving and selfless; the food that they prepared for us was exotic and piquant. Passion fruit, mango, Santo Domingo coffee, and home-cooked meals consumed our appetites. Even in difficult conditions, the pastor and his wife showed me the extent of human sacrifice and strength of character.

My experience in the Dominican Republic summarizes my action movie. The encouragement of my peers, my zeal for God, and the will to serve during this time spurred me into action, which was translated through my broken Spanish accent and sweat-laden movements in their service.

As an eleventh grader at present, I have learned to embrace the commonplace day-to-day experiences. School is never easy, but I put my best effort into every new challenge that I face. I had many instances of failure, remember countless hours of studying, and made difficult sacrifices, but these bumps in the road only led to a smooth and promising destination. I am a very persistent and driven individual. As the youngest of three children, I wanted to prove that I could accomplish everything on my own and achieve greatness; however, my family and the friends that I have met along the way have shown me that it takes mutual effort and dependence to feel complete, whole, and truly satisfied. I thank God for all of the people and experiences he has placed within my life, for He is the director and creator of my movie. Through all of the memorable, spontaneous experiences that have left a mark on my life, I can produce a real-life movie masterpiece, and it plays on infinitely.

"A Tale to Tell"
Brian Park

"If you're a dreamer, come in. If you're a dreamer, a wisher, a liar. A hope-er, a pray-er, a magic bean buyer... If you're a pretender, come sit by my fire. For we have some flax-golden tales to spin. Come in! Come in!"
-Shel Silverstein

All of us have a tale to tell. Just imagine that every one of us is like a book, constantly jotting down words based on our thoughts and actions from the moment we are born to the day we take our last breath. During our lives we get a chance to tell others of the adventures we ventured on, the moments of joy, times when we all felt hopeless, and times such as when we are tempted into eating all the snacks in the cabinet (wasn't me). Such stories are then held onto by the listener until he or she dies or when he/she decide to pass it on. The prologue of my story begins in the city of Fukuoka, Japan with a certain woman at 2:00AM in the morning.....

It was 2:00AM in the morning when my mother felt a sudden pain in her stomach. She had been pregnant for 38 weeks now, and had assumed that it would take a few more weeks until the baby would be ready to arrive. Nevertheless, the pain continued to grow, and she called a taxi. In those days, my parents didn't have a car and my father was in Europe as a church missionary. She was rushed to the hospital and readied herself for the pain she was about to go through. She had already had her first child 2 years ago and knew how painful the birthing process was. The night was particularly hot, as it was in the middle of summer. During this night of July 25, 1994, at exactly 3:40 AM, a baby's cry rang out through the hallways of the hospital. Je Song Fujino Park, the first son and male in the Park family, had just been born. My story begins here.

I was born a few weeks premature, so I had to stay in the hospital for a few days after my birth. When I look back at those pictures of my first moments, I must say that I looked like a potato with hair and eyes. I was surprisingly tanner and tinier then my older sister had been, so my mother took care of me until I looked healthier. I remember being an observant child during my earlier years, absorbing everything I saw around me.

Thinking back, it must have been an amazing change, one moment you're in the womb with nothing to see and the next thing you know, you're seeing color and motion. You could leave me on the couch for hours as a child and I wouldn't budge, staring into space until I eventually fell asleep. I assume that this observant behavior soon led to the way I would view the way of the world philosophically.

After living for three years in Japan, my mother decided to stay in Korea for a few months for church reasons. This is where I met my grandparents in Korea for the first time. I remember vague moments during the time, the clearest one being when my tiny hands got a hold on a carton of eggs, after which my grandmother punished me. I remember my grandmother only through faint bits of memories, but I saw that she was a strong woman at heart. I understood how hard life had been for her to raise 5 children in the countryside (through the stories my father told), where you had to work all day to have food in your mouth. My grandfather on the other hand was a man of pride and love for his family. I remember him as a gentle figure in my vault of memories, and as someone who always smiled. I stayed with my grandparents for 6 months in total, and then moved to my next 3 year destination: Denmark.

Before I begin with my story in Denmark, let me talk a little bit about how my church affected my life. My church began to affect my life from the moment I was born; being that my father was a pastor. I was taught wrong from right and the principles of life that I follow to this day. My church was a Family Church, a small church that focused on bringing all religions of the world together. The motto that our church focuses on is "One Family Under God" and hence, we believe that our goal is to unite everybody in the world based not on their beliefs, but on their way of life.

My father was a pastor and a church missionary at the time in Denmark, so we lived for a few years in the church he was working in. I remember the cozy little room that we were given and all the generous people that also inhabited the church. To me the church ground was an enormous world that was all mine to explore. I remember always wandering about the church in search of adventures, such as searching the yard of the church for any interesting bugs or going to the kitchen to watch Rosie the chef batching up the meal of the day, or perhaps sneaking upstairs to see if her son Daniel had stashed any snacks in an

unconcealed spot. During this time of exploration, my little sister was born and a year afterwards, my brother. My parents then decided to take us on a trip all across Europe for sightseeing with my grandparents. After we visited many places around Europe such as Italy, Greece, Rome, Paris, and Sweden, my family then packed up and moved to the land of the free and opportunity, America.

America mystified me even before I began living there. To me, America was a country that was big, powerful and run by the Native Americans (I think this was due to a misinterpreted statement by one of church members). At first I cried, telling my parents I didn't want to go live in a teepee with a bunch of Native Americans running around. After my parents reassured me that there were no "Indians", we finally moved. Perhaps the most mysterious thing about my plane ride to America was losing the ability to speak Danish – not to say I was fluent, but I wasn't exactly a beginner. Now I can only say a few words, such as "kaneu"(knife) and "gigaf"(giraffe) which is pretty much useless. But now I had to face the challenges of learning English and adapting to a new environment.

I wish I could say that life was easy in America. Unfortunately, that wasn't the case. When I began to go to school, things were not only chaotic but I was also pretty much an outcast. Let's look at the first day of school in a play format shall we?

Narrator: It's a warm day in September 11, 2001, summer vacation has just ended and kids are beginning to come into the auditorium and settle down. A lone boy sits in the corner of the back row, tears streaming down his face. It's his first day of 1st grade and he has no idea where to go. A teacher finally notices him and walks over....

Teacher: Hello Dear, are you ok?
Boy: ......
Teacher: Do you know where you're supposed to go?
Boy: ......
Teacher: Hmm, do you speak English?
Boy: (shakes head)
Teacher: I see, well you can follow me upstairs. Come, come.
Boy: (follows the teacher, with tears still flowing)

Narrator: The lone boy is led to his classroom where he has to introduce himself. He combines all his knowledge of English and attempts to speak.

Boy: Nice to meet you, I am Yu.
(Kids giggle)
Teacher: Repeat that please, this time louder
Boy: Nice to meet you, I am Yu.
Class: Hey Yu (giggles)
Teacher: Good Yu, you can sit right by the window.
Boy: (red-faced, rushes to his seat and begins to worry about what he said wrong)

Narrator: A few minutes later, a sinister event horrifies our protagonist...

Teacher: ...and so I will need you to bring 2 notebooks, 1 box of crayons, and-

Loudspeaker: This is an emergency announcement; all teachers please take your students to the main lobby to be taken home. Students who are unable to contact their parents will be kept in the auditorium. Also, children…
(Man runs into the room)

Man: Jackie, the World Trade Center just got hit. Doesn't your brother…..?
Teacher: (Trying to calm herself) Alright kids, pack up and line up outside the hallway.
Boy: (steps outside and sees a building on fire on a television set in a school)
Teacher: Shut that off! Shut that off!

Now you understand the bad start I had in America. Not only that, but also because I had lived in such a safe and kind community before coming to America, I felt that my mind would not be able to handle it all. It was like releasing a domestic animal into the wilderness. I was not sure how to act or feel. I wanted to adapt to this new environment that I had been introduced to, but at the same time didn't know how to (or just didn't want to). During this time I underwent a transformation that would continue to shape what I am today.

All changes, even the most longed for, have their melancholy; for what we leave behind us is a part of ourselves; we must die to one life before we can enter another.
~Anatole France

5 years later…

"JeSong? Get up JeSong you're going to be late for school."
I woke with a start, stretching to get all my muscles back in gear. Through my dazed eyes, I grabbed my glasses and looked up at the clock to see what time it was. At first, I thought the short hand was past 7, and then I realized it was 6:30. I groaned, as it was typical of my mother to wake me up an hour earlier than

usual. Today wasn't even a special day, just a normal freezing Monday on the 14th of January. I looked down at the floor, just thinking to myself how cold it must be. "A few more minutes wouldn't hurt," I mumbled as I reburied myself in the coziness of my blanket. I was just about to doze off when the door to my room opened and my mother walked in.

"JeSong get up, you're going to miss the bus." she repeated, more urgently this time. "Mph" I muttered, and this time I quickly got to my feet and ran into the bathroom. I washed my face to get rid of any fatigue that was still stubbornly clinging to my face. Afterwards, I ran back to my room and changed my clothes. The clothes were freezing when I put them on, and I shivered slightly, but proceeded to make my bed and walk towards the dinner table. My mom had prepared a bowl of oatmeal for my breakfast, and as soon as I sat down, I began to quickly eat it to get the warmth of it. My mother was sitting across from me, talking to my older sister about something. After she finished with her, she turned her attention to me and started asking me questions, which I answered between bites of my oatmeal: Did you do all your homework? (yes, mom) Did you wash your face? (Yep) Did you make your bed? (of course).

I finished eating before she could ask any more question, and quickly grabbed my bag. "I'll be going now, Mom," I called as I put my shoes on. "Okay, see you later," she said as she walked up to the door. I opened the doors and felt the wave of cold air hit. I shivered, and then walked out.

As you can see in this short memory sequence, my mother cares deeply for me. Almost everyday, the same procedure would take place (minus the oatmeal). My mother would always be protective towards all her children and is always there to support us. Another thing you may notice in this memory sequence is my behavior. This is around the time I began to become Americanized. This started to affect the way I thought and acted towards others (such as putting my hands in my pocket while talking to an elder and not answering with the appropriate "neh" – honorific form of "yes" used toward adults). My relationship with my mother didn't change much, but my relationship with my father changed drastically. Let's look at another memory sequence.

April 18, 2005

I was having a great time at the moment. I mean 3 hours of video gaming and a bag of candy that was the size of my head?

Nothing was better than this (except perhaps, a big cup of parfait) and the fact that I had finished all my homework left me with a feeling of freedom. I was just about to lay back and get started when my father walked into the room. My father was a strongly built man, having served in the military when he was young (did I also mention he was a squad leader?). Hence, he also followed a strict disciplinary code and made sure that his family also followed it. As soon as he saw me playing, he rushed over and shut the TV off.

I stared at him dumbfounded. I had just been in a state of bliss, and here was my father, ending it all.

"What was that for!?" I shouted at him. He stared at me with stern eyes, eyeing the game controller and the candy bag. "Did you finish all your homework?" he asked, not breaking his glare. "Of course I did!" I answered back, upset that he didn't ask the question before he had acted. "If you finished your homework, why don't you go study or read a book?" he replied. With growing anger, I shouted at him, "Why can't I have my own time once in a while!? He snorted, clearly looking at me as a child that did not understand the ways of the world. "Right now, you don't understand, but you'll come to regret the moments you played when you could have studied." He simply replied before walking out of the room, leaving me in a furious mood. I decided to put it out of my mind and turned to television back on to try to reenter my moment of bliss. I never did.

As you can see, my father was a stern man who expressed his love for me by disciplining me every chance he got (this was just a minor incident compared to usual conflicts). My younger self did not yet understand this, and just believed that my father was constantly harassing me just for the fun of it. Therefore, I came to loathe my father, constantly avoiding him if possible. As I aged however, I began to understand my father's motives and how he really felt. However, another thing that greatly displeased him was my assimilating, as he viewed Americans as rude and selfish. We continued to clash over the years, sometimes over the smallest problems. I have to say, though, that our relationship has gotten slightly better over the years.

While I was growing up in America, I went to Japan numerous times, sometimes just for vacations or to help my grandmother maintain her house. Every time I went to Japan, I felt like I had

come home, that America was just a long vacation and that my real home was in Japan. However, I began to long for Korea, my fatherland. It didn't make sense to me that I was able to experience one home country, yet couldn't do the same with the other. It was like being able to see one parent, but unable to see the other. I asked my parents why I couldn't go to Korea, and they answered by replying that it wasn't the right time. I was curious to know what they meant by the "right time", but I shrugged it off and waited. Finally the right time arrived.

June 30, 2008

"We are going to Japan and Korea." Such were the words that I heard being spoken in my household. I was beyond excitement, yet felt nervous and mystified at the same time. It was more than 12 years since I last visited Korea, and to me, Korea was shrouded with dark curtains. I thought to myself, "Is it time to finally pull back the curtains?" I wasn't sure now that I knew we were going. My Korean wasn't the best and I was afraid that I might accidently offend my relatives. "Look at yourself." I thought. "Afraid to meet your own relatives! They were family to you 12 years ago and that's not going to change." Having built up the confidence, I went to prepare my things for the trip.

When I finally went to Korea, I was perplexed by everything. To me, Korea had been my Grandfather's house since I had never really gone outside when I was young. But what I experienced then changed everything I had thought about it. I saw the most intriguing things, heard the most fascinating music, and tasted the most delicious food. Yet through this entire experience only one thought lingered in my mind: I was home. The missing puzzle had finally been found. How I felt cannot be described in words (and yes, I checked the thesaurus and the dictionary). It was a magical feeling, finally experiencing Japan and Korea together. It was so magical that it made my trip to Disney World (gasp) seem boring.

When I finally returned home, I underwent another transformation. High school was only a month away and since middle school had ended in failure, I wanted to turn over a new leaf. This is also around the time I started to develop an identity in myself by finding the types of music, literature, sport, and interests, etc. that I enjoyed. It was a Golden Age for me, since I

had pretty much been a person who had gone with the flow. I even changed my name to Brian, to prove that I was a new me, not the quiet and shy boy from before. When high school finally came I was surprised at what a difference a little change in attitude could do. I made sure not to repeat the same mistakes that I had made in the past, and since past mistakes still haunted me, I made up for them by improving myself. Finally, a day came when I saw an opportunity to truly test whether I had changed or not. I was about to do something that would have made younger self squirm and run away in fear. I was going to run for school president.

At first, the idea seemed crazy to me. Me? Run for president? The idea seemed absurd, if not impossible. Yet, the more I thought about it, the more it seemed possible. I was running, not to prove to the school that I was some kid trying to get popularity, but to prove to myself that deep inside me, there was a part of me that was still asleep that I needed to awaken. When I began the campaign, I was a nervous wreck, messing up my opening speech and debate with stuttering and strange wording. I imagined I must have looked ridiculous up there, but to me, I was making my point. At the end, I lost, but to me it was a win.

The fact that I had just run for president was all the proof I needed to tell myself that I had changed. In the end, the winner came up to me to congratulate me on campaign. He told me that he had liked the certain fire that he saw within me and wished to give me a cabinet position. This came as a total surprise to me, since I hadn't been expecting an offer for a position. I quickly replied that I would be happy to take the position, and hence Jesong Park became the new Chancellor of EWSIS.

After becoming Chancellor, I began to attend meetings afterschool. I was able to meet up with other leaders of the school and discuss different issues with them. I've never been a fan of politics, but I soon came to enjoy the meetings. Another thing that was going on back at home was that I had applied for a youth program called KAYAC that takes young Korean-Americans to Korea to experience their homeland. I immediately applied for it, and after months of anxious waiting, news finally arrived that I had been accepted into the program. I was overjoyed, knowing that I would be able to experience Korea once more.

When I think back about how much I've changed since I had

first come to America, I have mixed feelings. Did I truly give up a part of myself in order to blend into this country of America? Should I have made a different decision on that day? All these questions come flooding into my head the more I think about it. Could my story have taken a more dramatic twist if I had never moved to America? I would never find out, but one thing I do know is that my story continues here. No matter where I go or what I do, my story would go on with me until the day I die. And to tell you the truth, my story has only just begun.

"My Brother and Me"
April Myung

I remember being told that my brother was Autistic for the first time.

My parents had called two younger sisters and my thirteen year-old self to the kitchen, where the drab linoleum flooring with its defeated, tattered edges seemed to reflect the quiet despair and defeat in my parents' eyes. Unaware of the reason why my sisters and I had been called, I worried the end of my ponytail, wondering if I had been caught trying on my mother's lipstick and was about to be scolded. However, I now believe that deep down inside, despite having been of an age in which my main concerns were frivolous in nature, I had realized that my parents' eyes were far too sorrowful for them to be delivering something as trivial as discipline. After a moment's pause, my mother took a deep, shuddering breath, and in a voice that did not sound like her own, said, "Ne-Ne is Autistic."

It was the breathing that I first noticed. The breaths of everyone in the room were different. Mine was initially a deep exhalation of relief. I had not been caught. I started to grin and give a smug smile to my younger sisters when I finally processed that the deep shuddering breaths were the sounds of my parents trying to restrain their tears. That was when I started to wonder what "Ne-Ne is Autistic" meant. Ne-Ne, whose birth certificate reads: Derek Myung, is my adorable younger brother, who was three years old at the time. He was a docile and somewhat reticent child, adored by the entire family for his sweet personality and soft demeanor. However, when all the words in his vocabulary could be counted on one hand as a three year old, my parents grew worried and took him to the doctor. After extensive testing with several therapists, he was diagnosed with Autism. As my parents calmed themselves down

and tried to explain what being Autistic entailed to my sisters and me, I started to fret and have shameful thoughts. After initially being concerned for my brother and wondering if he had a future and would ever be able to be independent as an adult, I started to selfishly wonder what would happen to our family.

My family comprises of seven family members: my mother (Yoojung Jeon), my father (Nosung Myung), my grandmother (Jungyoon Jeon), my fifteen year-old sister (Heidi Myung), my seven year-old sister (Irene Myung), and my six year-old brother (Derek Myung). As expected of a large family in a moderately sized home, our daily household life is generally noisy, messy, and downright raucous at times. Although this chaotic environment often makes it quite difficult to focus on my studies, I am grateful for the noise and energy, as I am never lonely. I am so accustomed to the ever present noise that is a consequence of my large family that I find silence to be "louder" than noise.

A typical day as the eldest child of my household consists of a variety of duties and activities. As a Korean-American, I have the distinct boon – and bane at times – of living a lifestyle that is of two, nearly polar, cultures. Fort Lee, the town that I was raised in and its large white and Korean population (62.75%-white, 16.85%-Korean) only served to exacerbate the clashing lifestyles present in my life. Therefore, my aforementioned chores and activities varied in a similar fashion. I had to take my siblings to the playground to "develop their social skills", set up the dinner table for my parents, babysit, mow the lawn, and shovel the snow. Whenever I complained to my friends, as I was apt to do whenever my chores took a toll on my body, my Korean friends would be puzzled by the fact that my parents made me "waste" time that I could spend studying on outside chores, such as mowing the lawn, and my non-Asian friends would often be bewildered by the fact that a girl, even if she was the eldest child of the family, had to do the more physically strenuous tasks that I had.

I often had difficulty trying to align the different impulses I had with the varying situations I was in. I remember the family barbeques that my family and I frequent to this day, and how in those days, where the scent of meat and freshly cut grass permeated the air, I had to be docile and obedient. I would give my best impression of the filial daughter, listening to the conversations between the adults attentively and suppressing any "rude" impulse to act in a childish and unruly manner. On the other hand, my

American friends and their parents were puzzled by the meek mannerisms that I initially displayed as a youth, and I eventually learned that, as with clothing, mannerisms had to be fitted to each culture. Many of my non-Korean friends in elementary and middle school had difficulty understanding how I prioritized my life as a Korean American. I remember disappointing quite a few friends and even alienating some (when I was too young to explain myself) by missing birthday parties and other similar events after refusing to argue with my mother when she said no. It was not until I was in middle school that I realized that it was not my friends who were the misunderstanding ones, but I who was unable to understand, as I was asking my friends to understand that filial duties were a more of Korean culture without explaining it to them.

As I gradually learned to share my two cultures, I also was able to appreciate and respect those of my peers. Being cognizant of other cultures thus a little more enabled me to become aware of the profound racism that was prevalent within my motherland, Korea, when I visited

Korea for the first time in twelve years in 2008 with my mountain climbing group. I had already gone mountain climbing with the NYAC (New York Alpine Club) for the summer before in Utah and was in the midst of developing an ardor for mountain climbing and hiking that would last to this day. Utah had been beautiful, with its untainted wildlife, hiking trails with stunning views, and challenging mountains to climb. I had been awestruck by the experience of hiking to the summit of Mt. Timpanagos (15 mile hike up) and was eager to go climbing again in Korea. I was not disappointed and hiked three mountains and mountain climbed/belayed for three days. I could confidently say that the hike up Sulak Mountain was one of the most physically, mentally, and emotionally strenuous actions I had ever taken.

During this two day hike, I was in a constantly alert state as the slippery rocks and trail made it hazardous and easy to twist an ankle, as one unfortunate member of the group had. However, despite the difficulty of the hike, the breathtaking view on top of Sulak Mountain, surrounded by cloud enshrouded mountains of a similar height, along with the euphoria of reaching the peak after physically and

mentally testing my bounds with my colleagues made everything worth it. This experience made it possible for me to discover my ability to endure, persevere, and break down difficult jobs into smaller, more palatable ones in order to achieve my goals. It also filled me with the need to find more "pieces of myself", pushing me to challenge myself in unfamiliar environments to discover other interests. I am grateful to my mother for encouraging me to take a risk and sign up for this unusual summer camp rather than simply lying around at home with the TV as my main source of diversion.

After the cathartic experience of climbing several mountains and going on several three day hiking excursions in which we pitched tents in the chilly niches near the peaks of mountains, I was refreshed. Filled with the love that nature lovers would recognize and associate with a long stay surrounded by nothing but nature, I went down from the mountains and stayed in the homes of several close relatives for two weeks before returning to the Unites States. I was thrilled. I was finally able to match faces to the voices that I had made long distance calls to once a month and was ecstatic. On the first day of my stay with my relatives, I met my father's immediate family and listened to their stories. They understood that my Korean was weak, as I had attended Korean weekend school in the United States for about two years before quitting, and made an effort to use simple words. I got to listen to my grandmother (from my father's side) regale me with tales of how she had grown up in the Korean province of Choongcheongnamdo and my grandfather speak about his days in the province of Changwon. I listened with a grain of salt to an uncle tell me with a mischievous smile that the "Myungs are of royal blood, as we are descendants of members of the Ming dynasty, who fled to South Korea when they were overthrown by the Ming dynasty." I also fell in love with my sweet cousins, who took time out of their busy schedules as students to show me more of their country and my motherland.

However, despite how enamored I was of this innovative, clean, and remarkable country, I could not ignore the racism that plagued this wonderful nation. This country, which boasted the latest in technology, was still bogged down by half a century old division. This beautiful nation, whose display of hospitality shown to me by many Korean strangers who recognized my accent, stunned me in its inability to sign a peace treaty with its other half, North Korea. Although North and South Koreans shared the same ancestors and had once lived on the same soil, the Korean DMZ (demilitarized zone) separates these nations and forces

soldiers that share the same ancestry to shoot at one another.

I was dismayed by the hatred that some of the children displayed towards North Koreans, as all of the children, upon my asking them, had told me that they had never, in fact, met a North Korean. However, what truly upset me was the logistical facts that my friend presented to me when I visited Korea the following summer with KAYAC (Korean American Youth Assistance Coalition), as she had told me that the unification of North Korea and South Korea was simply not possible.

We have been fortunate enough to get into KAYAC (a highly competitive program to get into that involved an application process, essay, test, and interview that introduces the members to their motherland by showing them and explaining to them national landmarks, symbols, and culture) and were discussing the viability of the two Koreas reuniting in our lifetime. Although I wanted to believe in the possibility of the ideal situation of North Korean and South Korean families that had been split apart by the border reuniting, I couldn't help but be disheartened by the logically sound argument that my friend, Susan, had provided. The mountain of obstacles, which ranged from economic to political to prejudice issues, made the unification of North Korea and South Korea seem far away and unattainable, indeed. However, after being blessed with opportunities to learn about South Korea and its attempts to reunify with North Korea, I made the decision to contribute even in the smallest ways, by raising awareness of the irrationality of prejudice towards North Koreans (which I had previously been guilty of) amongst my own peers.

That same summer, my parents gave me the opportunity to go on a missions trip to Tanzania, Africa. There, with 7 other missionaries, I volunteered at an orphanage, interacted with Tanzanian students my age, and witnessed extreme poverty. This trip was a life altering experience in more ways than one. I will never stop being thankful for the chance that I had to go to this nation. I am especially thankful for having been able to visit the high school that Isaac had attended and the orphanage that Dorothy had lived in.

In one of the high schools of Dar Es Salam, the capital of Tanzania, I met Isaac. He was a nineteen year old Tanzanian who was easily a foot taller than my 5'3" frame. A single conversation with him is what fuels me with the motivation that I require to work so hard to achieve my

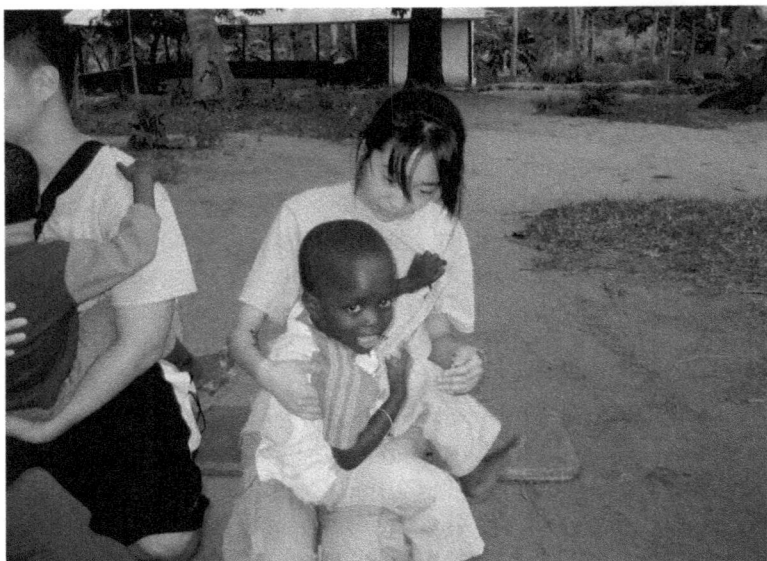

goal of contribute to the field of Autism. You see, Isaac was blessed with both an insatiable desire to learn and a refreshingly direct personality. After speaking to high school classes, my missions group always spoke to the students for around an hour before leaving. When Isaac came up to me, he asked me what my favorite topic was in school. When I answered by saying, "Chemistry," he asked me what my favorite recent developments in the field of chemistry was. When I was unable to answer, he looked me in the eyes and said, "Listen April. You are blessed. You have so many opportunities available at your fingertips. Learn and change someone's life!" I decided that I would. After 5 minutes of conversation, I promised the lean student with the fiery eyes that I would make use of the opportunities that he craved for and make a difference in one family member's life: my baby brother Derek.

At the orphanage, I met a young girl named Dorothy. She was captivating. Despite her raggedy dress, which was stained with what appeared to be a week's worth of meals, and her tousled hair, her clear and beautiful eyes and honest smile floored me. I could not understand how a child who had never had the luxuries that I had taken for granted could be filled with such unadulterated happiness. That was when I realized how corrupt I had become. I realized that I had come to associate material wealth with happiness and had become unable to be "happy" without spending money in some respect. I realized that my true moments of happiness was when I was able to push myself and find new aspects of myself to share with the friends and family that I had come to treasure in my seventeen years of living. And I realized why I had thought this young Tanzanian orphan was familiar; my younger brother, Derek possessed the same, clear eyes. That was what solidified my decision to make making a significant contribution to the field of Autism the primary focus of my life.

Upon coming back to the United States, I immediately commenced searching for a volunteering position at the Autism therapeutic nursery where my brother had improved so significantly. There, at the Jewish Community Center, I volunteered on Sundays, serving as a

teacher's assistant to a class of severely autistic children whose ages ranged from six to eight. I was shocked by how understaffed the facilities were and realized that it was due to the free and voluntary nature of the program, whereas my brother was enrolled in the weekly and highly exorbitant classes that my town's special education department helped pay the tuition for. I threw myself into this job and decided to devote myself to this program and was pleased with the results. After half a year of careful teaching, in which I asked for advice from Derek's therapists, several of the students, namely Jonathan, Neil, and Kunal improved significantly enough for the teacher to notice. Jonathan, who had initially been prone to beating his head with his fists when he was upset at least once every class, had reduced his tantrums by half and sat still when he was angry instead. Neil no longer compulsively ate the lunches of his companions except on his few contrary days, and Kunal could now exchange a few words with both me and the teacher.

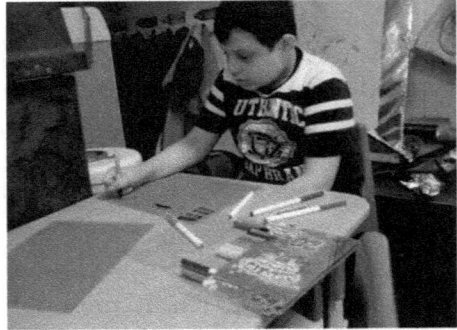

Inspired by Isaac and Dorothy, I also started searching for an independent research topic and sought the guidance of the teacher in charge of the stem cell research lab in Bergen County Academies, Mrs. Donna Leonardi. Although many of my peers in the lab found their topic within a month and often jokingly teased me for not finding one months into the process, I continued to search for an inspiration for a topic. To clarify, my main issue was not mainly a lack of inspiration but the lack of information to form a thesis on. As is common knowledge, there are no proven causes and solutions to Autism. Therefore, I had no leads to go upon. However, after 6 months of going into the stem cell lab's online subscriptions to medical publications, I finally conceived the idea of lowering the levels of Nitric oxide in a model cell of Autism by raising the levels of glucose with Sodium valproate. Here is the abstract of the research paper that I submitted to the New Jersey Regional Science Fair and won The Best *in vitro* Award for:

Autism is a severe developmental disorder whose prevalence rises exponentially, and despite years of research into the pathophysiology of Autism, a cause remains elusive. Nitric oxide (NO), a free radical known to affect neurodevelopment, has been implicated as a potential cause of Autism. Although the cause of the high levels of NO found in Autism is unknown, a consequence of high concentrations of NO is the heightened production of tumor necrosis factor-α (TNF-α), a cytokine implicated in many autoimmune diseases. After finding a study that lowered levels of NO within cells with high levels of glucose and another that reported Sodium valproate (VPA) as a potent inhibitor of glucose transport, I decided to try to lower levels of NO and TNF-α with VPA. In this project, the potential of VPA's inhibitory effect will be explored by experimenting with its effect on TNF-α and NO production. It is hypothesized that if the levels of VPA in the cell culture medium are increased, levels of glucose will increase in a dose-dependent manner, causing levels of NO production and consequently TNF-α to decrease. Using NO and TNF-α ELISAs, it was found that .10M VPA had the optimum results, lowering the levels of both NO and TNF-α within the astrocytes significantly ($p<0.05$). Since the VPA proved to be limited but successful, it may have applications in the treatment of Autism. Future research would entail experimentation with other methods of inhibiting glucose transport for more successful results.

I am glad that I have found a passion in medical research and am thankful to Derek for being the main trigger to my research and interest in Autism. However, "curing" him is no longer my goal. I had initially thought that before having an Autistic brother, my family and I had lived happily, blithely unaware and unconcerned about special education, thinking that it was an issue separate from "us", the "normal"

people. I had also thought that we were now suffering from other people's indifference when the town gave my family a hard time about providing us with funding for Derek's education. I was also paranoid about anyone looking down on my brother and selfishly tried to compensate for and hide his slow language development. But I did not realize that his innately friendly and innocent nature would help him make friends, and that Autism, once he learned to handle it, was not a disorder to worry about and something to be cured from, but another component of Derek's lovable personality. After six blessed years with Derek, I learned that Autism is a trait that is like a garrulous personality – one just needed to learn how to handle one's own personality – and got to find a goal that I had a passion for: how to help others learn to handle their Autism, not cure it.

www.ingramcontent.com/pod-product-compliance
Lightning Source LLC
Chambersburg PA
CBHW020703270326
41928CB00005B/249